Children's
PLANET EARTH
Encyclopedia

Jen Green

PaRragon

Bath · New York · Singapore · Hong Kong · Cologne · Delhi · Melbourne

First published in 2008
Parragon
Queen Street House
4 Queen Street
Bath BA1 1HE, UK

Copyright © Parragon 2008

Author: Jen Green
Consultant: John Williams
This edition produced by Tall Tree Ltd, London

ISBN 978-1-4075-1310-2

2—

Children's
PLANET EARTH
Encyclopedia

Contents

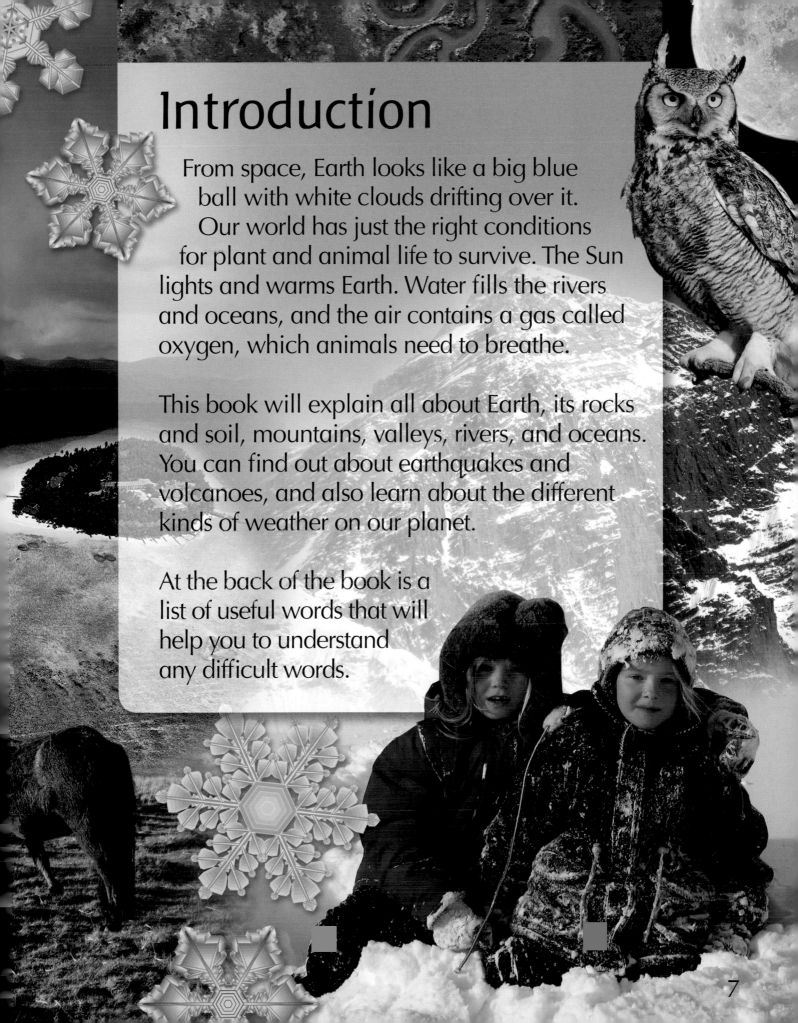

Introduction

From space, Earth looks like a big blue ball with white clouds drifting over it. Our world has just the right conditions for plant and animal life to survive. The Sun lights and warms Earth. Water fills the rivers and oceans, and the air contains a gas called oxygen, which animals need to breathe.

This book will explain all about Earth, its rocks and soil, mountains, valleys, rivers, and oceans. You can find out about earthquakes and volcanoes, and also learn about the different kinds of weather on our planet.

At the back of the book is a list of useful words that will help you to understand any difficult words.

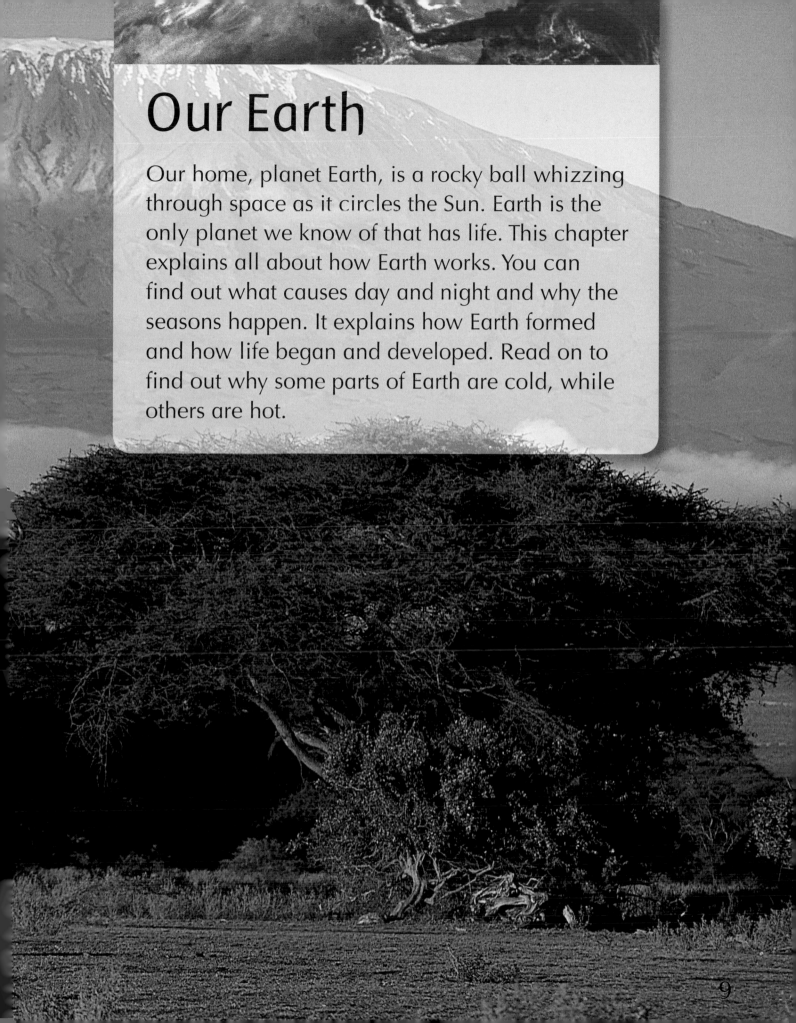

Our Earth

Our home, planet Earth, is a rocky ball whizzing through space as it circles the Sun. Earth is the only planet we know of that has life. This chapter explains all about how Earth works. You can find out what causes day and night and why the seasons happen. It explains how Earth formed and how life began and developed. Read on to find out why some parts of Earth are cold, while others are hot.

Our solar system

Earth is one of nine planets circling the Sun. The Sun, its nine planets, and smaller rocks make up a family called the solar system. Earth and the other planets follow paths called orbits as they circle the Sun.

The planets

Earth is the third planet from the Sun, after Mercury and Venus. Earth is the fifth-biggest planet, but all the planets are tiny compared to the Sun.

Sun

Mercury

Venus

Earth

Mars

Jupiter

The Sun

The Sun is our local star. It is an enormous fiery ball shooting light and heat in all directions. The Sun's rays light and heat Earth. Without the Sun's warmth and energy, no living things could survive on Earth.

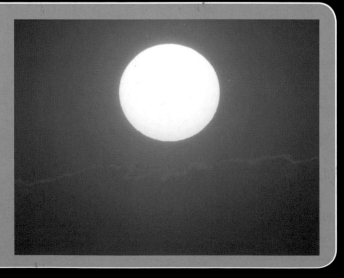

10

Earth

Earth looks blue from space because it is mainly covered by oceans. The equator is an imaginary line that divides Earth into two halves called hemispheres. The poles are the places farthest north and south on Earth.

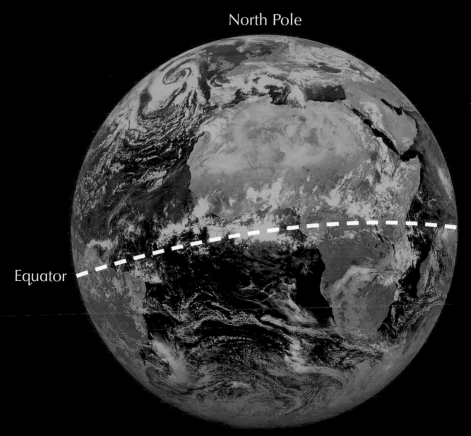

North Pole

Equator

South Pole

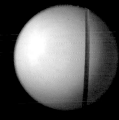

Saturn

Uranus

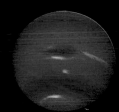

Neptune

Pluto

Stars

All the stars in the night sky are suns, like our Sun. Believe it or not, our Sun is just one of 100 billion stars in our part of the universe. Our Sun belongs to a huge group of stars called the Milky Way.

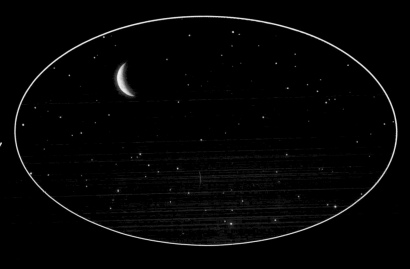

11

Spinning Earth

Earth seems still but, in fact, our world is spinning as it circles the Sun. This spin is called rotation. It takes 24 hours to complete one full rotation, which we call a day.

Day and night

Earth rotates around an imaginary line called the axis, which joins the north and south poles. When Earth turns into the sunlight, it is day where you live. When Earth turns out of the sunlight, it is night.

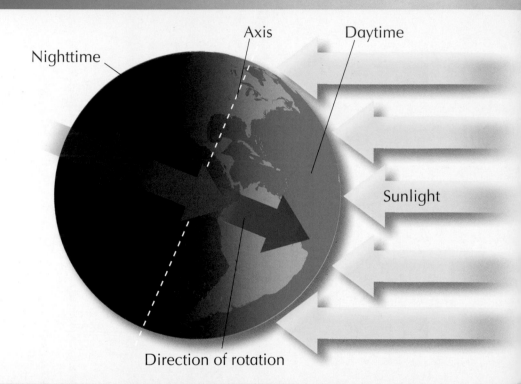

Nighttime

Axis

Daytime

Sunlight

Direction of rotation

Daytime

When the day begins, the Sun seems to rise in the east. It then moves across the sky and sets, or goes down, in the west. However, the Sun isn't really moving. Earth's rotation produces this effect.

When an object blocks the sunlight, it makes a shadow. When you wave, your shadow waves, too!

Nighttime

When it is dark, your part of Earth faces away from the Sun. The Moon and stars shine in the darkness. The Moon has no light of its own but is lit up by the Sun.

Active at night

People and many animals are awake and busy by day when the Sun shines and we can see clearly. We sleep at night when it's dark and we can't see much. Some animals, such as owls, hunt at night.

The owl's large eyes help it to hunt in dim light at dusk or by moonlight.

Earth's orbit

As you sit still reading this, Earth is racing on its orbit, or journey, around the Sun. It takes 365 days to complete one full orbit. We call this a year. Earth tilts, and this produces the regular changes we call the seasons.

Earth's tilt

Earth leans over as it rotates and orbits the Sun. This tilt carries you nearer or farther from the Sun at different times of year.

Axis

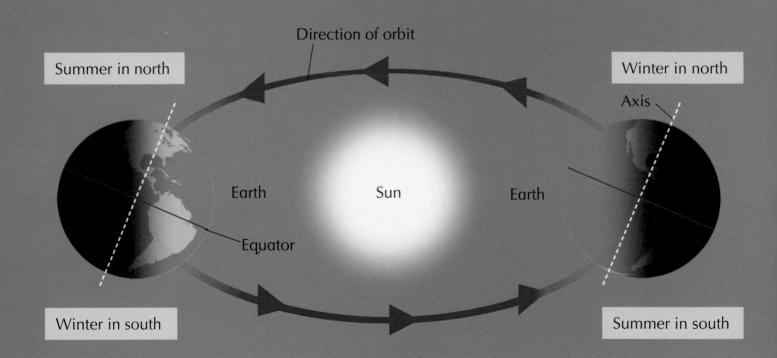

Direction of orbit

Summer in north

Winter in north

Axis

Earth

Sun

Earth

Equator

Winter in south

Summer in south

The seasons

As Earth orbits the Sun, the northern half leans toward the Sun and has summer. The southern half leans away and has winter. Six months later, Earth leans the opposite way, and the seasons are reversed.

DID YOU KNOW? The seasons are most noticeable at the poles. This is because these parts are most affected by Earth's tilt.

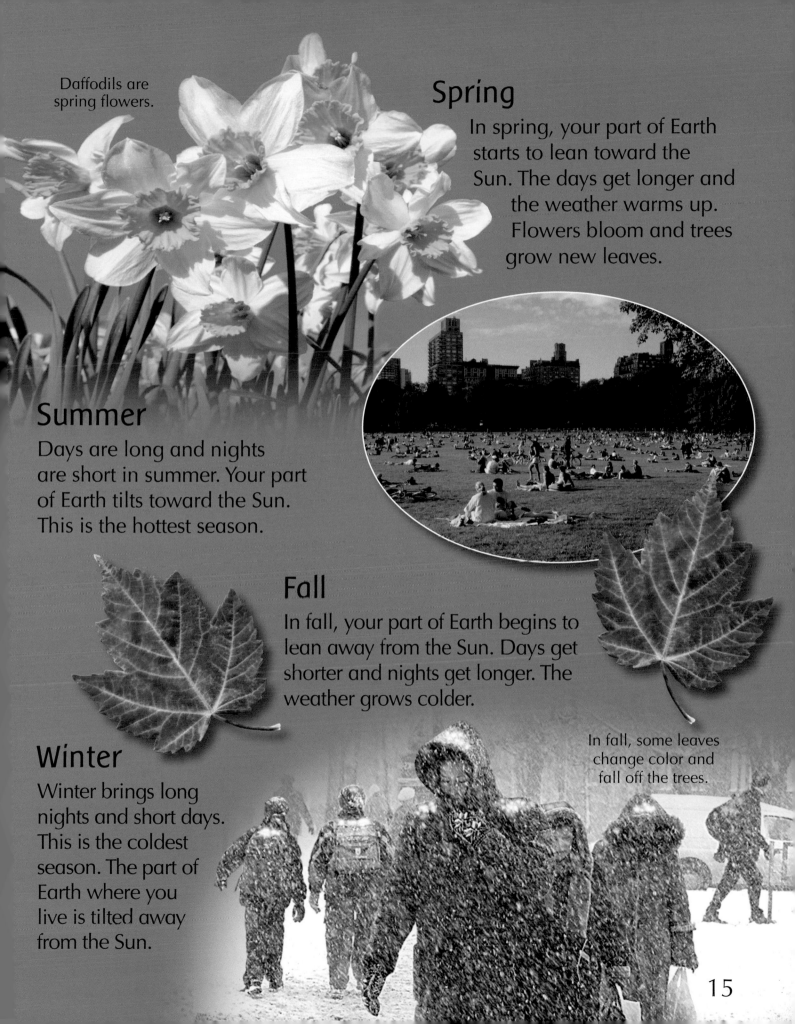

Daffodils are spring flowers.

Spring

In spring, your part of Earth starts to lean toward the Sun. The days get longer and the weather warms up. Flowers bloom and trees grow new leaves.

Summer

Days are long and nights are short in summer. Your part of Earth tilts toward the Sun. This is the hottest season.

Fall

In fall, your part of Earth begins to lean away from the Sun. Days get shorter and nights get longer. The weather grows colder.

In fall, some leaves change color and fall off the trees.

Winter

Winter brings long nights and short days. This is the coldest season. The part of Earth where you live is tilted away from the Sun.

15

Forces on Earth

Earth's huge size and weight make it pull objects toward it. This pull, called gravity, prevents you and everything else on Earth from flying off into space!

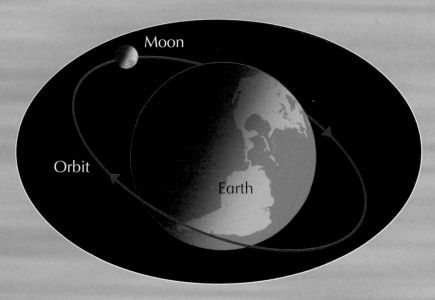

Moon

Orbit

Earth

The Moon

Earth's gravity keeps the Moon orbiting around it. The Moon also has gravity, which tugs at the oceans on Earth.

Gravity

Earth's gravity causes anything you drop to fall to the ground. All huge, heavy objects, such as planets, have gravity. The Sun's gravity is very strong. It keeps Earth and other planets in the solar system rotating around it.

DID YOU KNOW?

The area affected by a planet's magnetic pull is called its magnetic field. Earth's magnetic field stretches 37,300 miles (60,000 km) into space.

Magnetic pull

Scientists believe that iron inside Earth makes it magnetic—it acts like a giant bar magnet. The two ends of the magnet are the north and south poles. Earth's magnetic pull reaches far out into space.

Tiny pieces of iron called filings are pulled toward this bar magnet, showing its magnetic field.

Which way is north?

Earth's north and south poles have a very strong magnetic pull. A compass contains a magnetic needle that points to the north. It can be used to help people find their way if they are lost.

However high you jump on a trampoline, the pull of gravity will bring you back to Earth!

17

The Sun

How Earth formed

Earth is incredibly old. Scientists believe the
Sun and planets began to form about five billion
years ago. Our solar system developed from
a cloud of gas and dust spinning in space.

The solar system forms

Gas in the center of the spinning cloud formed
the Sun. Parts of dust stuck together to make rocks.
These crashed and stuck together to make rocky
planets, including Earth. Meanwhile, the Sun's
gravity kept the planets
rotating around it.

Pieces of rock orbiting
the Sun crashed
together to form larger
rocks and planets.

Early Earth

The young planet Earth was a fiery ball
of hot, liquid rock. The heat came from
all the rocks that had crashed together.
Heavy rocks sank to the planet's center.
Lighter rocks floated to the surface. There, they
gradually cooled to make a crust.

Rocks from space

The early Earth had no atmosphere to shield it from space. Giant rocks called meteorites crashed to the planet's surface. They made large hollows called craters.

Meteorite crater in Arizona.

Earth facts

- Earth's inside is still hot, liquid rock. The outside has cooled and hardened to make a solid crust.
- Earth is not perfectly round. It bulges slightly in the middle and is flatter at the poles.
- Earth is tiny compared to the Sun. You could fit more than a million Earths inside the Sun.

Volcanoes everywhere

About four billion years ago, Earth's surface was dotted with volcanoes (see pages 64–75) erupting hot lava. Gas and steam from the volcanoes formed Earth's first atmosphere. The steam formed clouds, which dropped rain. The water collected in hollows, which eventually became the oceans.

These bacteria are shown many times larger than actual size.

Life begins and changes

Scientists believe that life began on Earth about 3.8 billion years ago. Over millions of years, living things very slowly changed to suit their surroundings. These changes are called evolution.

First life

The first living things appeared in the oceans. They were tiny, simple creatures called bacteria, made of just one cell. Much later, tiny plants called algae developed in the sea.

Plants make oxygen

The algae used the Sun's energy to grow. They gave off oxygen. Some of these tiny plants grew in mounds called stromatolites. These mounds still grow in warm seas today.

Stromatolite mounds in Australia.

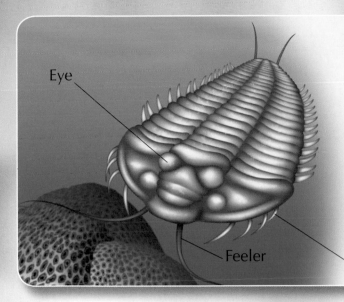

Animals appear

The first animals appeared in the oceans about 600 million years ago. They, too, were very simple creatures, with soft bodies. Gradually, animals developed more complicated bodies made up of many cells. Some, such as sea creatures called trilobites, developed hard shells.

Eye

Feeler

Trilobites had many legs.

Life moves onto land

About 400 million years ago, the first animals with backbones appeared. They were fish. Gradually, many different types of fish evolved. Some developed fleshy fins and crawled out of the water to live on land.

Mudskippers are fish that can move about on land.

DID YOU KNOW?

Trilobites were probably the first animals to have eyes. They also had feelers on their heads, which they used to search for food.

21

Fossils

Fossils are the remains of plants and animals that lived and died millions of years ago. The remains have been preserved, usually as rock. Scientists discover all about prehistoric life by studying fossils.

The hard shell of this ammonite has turned to rock.

Ammonite

This is a fossil of an ammonite. Ammonites were creatures with shells that swam in the oceans millions of years ago. The living animal had tentacles that stuck out of its coiled shell.

How ammonite fossils formed

When the ammonite died, it sank to the seabed. The soft parts rotted away, and the shell was buried by sand. Over millions of years, the sand slowly hardened into rock. Minerals seeped into the shell, until it, too, became rock.

Dead ammonite sank to the seabed.

Ammonite and sand slowly turned to rock.

Amber

Amber is a different kind of fossil. The clear, yellow material is fossilized tree resin—a sticky sap that oozed from prehistoric trees. Insects got trapped in the sap, which then hardened to make a fossil.

You can see the insects' delicate legs and wings in this fossil.

Amber fossils may be up to 90 million years old

Fossil fern

The print of a fern leaf has been preserved in this rock. Ferns like warm, damp conditions. They grew well in the steamy prehistoric forests 300 million years ago.

Prehistoric life

Since life began, many amazing animals have lived on Earth. We call the long period from 230 million years ago to 65 million years ago the Age of Reptiles. During this time, giant reptiles ruled the land, sky, and sea.

Tyrannosaurus Rex was a fierce meat-eating dinosaur.

Dinosaurs

A group of reptiles called dinosaurs were a terror on the land. There were many kinds of dinosaurs. Some were only as big as cats. Others were the size of jumbo jets. Some dinosaurs were meat eaters, while others ate only plants.

DID YOU KNOW?

The largest dinosaurs measured about 72 feet (22 m) long. The ground shook when they walked. The very biggest dinosaurs were plant eaters. There are no dinosaurs living today.

Plesiosaurs swam using their feet as paddles.

Swimming and flying reptiles

Other huge reptiles swam in the oceans. Plesiosaurs had long, snakelike necks and feet shaped like paddles. Another group of reptiles, the pterosaurs, soared through the skies on skin-covered wings.

Dinosaur fossils

This scientist is uncovering the skeleton of a dinosaur. He is chipping away the rock to reveal the fossil. Dinosaur bones have been found all over the world. Experts also find dinosaur tracks, and even dinosaur dung.

Dinosaurs die out

The dinosaurs and other giant reptiles died out 65 million years ago. Experts believe a giant meteorite, or space rock, smashed into Earth, causing a huge dust cloud to block the Sun for years. As a result, many plants died and there was not enough food for the dinosaurs.

The meteorite exploded when it hit Earth. The disaster made Earth's climate change suddenly.

Earth's climate

Climate is the regular pattern of weather.
Each part of Earth has its own climate.
The Sun has a big effect on the climate,
but so do mountains, the seas, and cities.

Heat from the Sun

The Sun's rays are overhead
or nearly overhead in the
region around the equator,
which has a hot, tropical
climate. At the poles, the
Sun's rays spread over a
wider area, so they have
less heating power. This
means that the poles have a
cold climate.

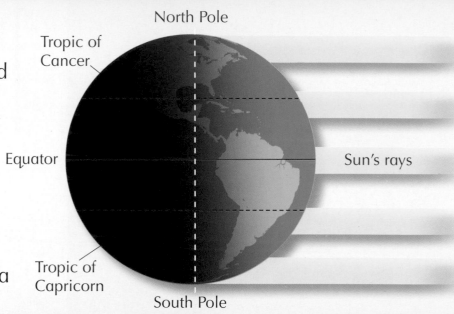

North Pole

Tropic of Cancer

Equator

Sun's rays

Tropic of Capricorn

South Pole

DID YOU KNOW?

The sea warms up and cools
down more slowly than
land, keeping temperatures
on the coast steady. Many
places far inland have very
hot summers and very cold
winters because they are far
from the sea.

Coastal climates

Many places by the sea have a mild climate.
Temperatures stay fairly steady there because sea
breezes cool the land in summer
and warm it in winter.

Cool heights

Mountains usually have a cold climate. The air high on mountains cannot hold as much of the Sun's heat as the air at sea level. The tops of high mountains are covered with ice and snow all year round.

Clouds bring rain to mountains.

City climates

Cities only cover a small area of the planet, but they have their own climate. Buildings and roads soak up the Sun's heat by day and give it out at night. This makes cities warmer than the nearby countryside.

Climate zones

A region's climate affects the plants and animals that live there. Large areas of Earth's surface have the same types of plants growing there. These regions are called biomes.

Earth's biomes

You can see the world's main biomes on this map. The types of plants that grow in each place depend on how warm it is and how much rain falls. Hot, rainy places have many types of plants. Fewer plants grow in cold or dry places.

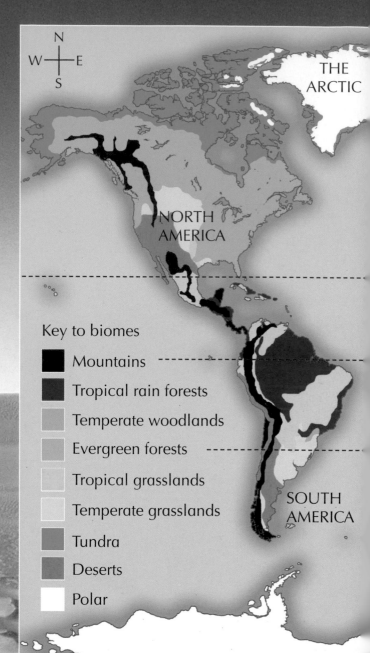

THE ARCTIC

NORTH AMERICA

Key to biomes

- Mountains
- Tropical rain forests
- Temperate woodlands
- Evergreen forests
- Tropical grasslands
- Temperate grasslands
- Tundra
- Deserts
- Polar

SOUTH AMERICA

Deserts

Deserts are very dry places where less than 10 inches (25 cm) of rain falls each year. Some deserts get no rain at all for years. Deserts may be sandy, rocky, or stony. Many are boiling hot by day and freezing cold at night.

EUROPE

ASIA

Tropic of
Cancer

AFRICA

Equator

Tropic of
Capricorn

AUSTRALASIA

ANTARCTICA

Temperate
woodland in fall.

Temperate zones

Temperate regions lie
between the poles and
the tropics and have
a mild, rainy climate.
In temperate woodlands,
most trees lose their
leaves in fall.

Cold forests and tundra

In the cold northern forests,
trees stay green all year. Little
grows in the icy tundra except
during the short summer.
The ground beneath the
surface stays frozen all year.

Plants bloom during the short
tundra summer.

Hot climates

Places on the equator and in the tropics have hot climates. It is warm there all year round, and nights are never frosty. Snow only falls on the tops of the very highest mountains.

Death Valley is a desert in the western United States.

Hottest places

Dallol in East Africa has the hottest average temperature on the planet—it stays at about 93°F (34°C). Death Valley has some of the highest temperatures ever recorded— up to 132.8°F (56°C)—but it does not stay that hot all the time.

Two seasons

Earth's tilt affects the tropics very little, so there is no spring, summer, fall, or winter. But some tropical places have two seasons— a dry and a rainy season.

India has its wet season from April to September every year.

Lush rain forests

Rain falls almost every day on most places at the equator. Rain forest trees love the hot, damp conditions. More types of plants and animals live in tropical rain forests than in any other biome.

Hot grasslands

Tropical grasslands grow in places that get less rain than rain forests but more rain than deserts. These areas are home to many grass-eating animals, such as zebras and antelopes, and the animals that feed on them, such as lions.

DID YOU KNOW?

In 1922, the city of Al Aziziyah in North Africa had the highest temperature ever recorded on Earth—an incredible 135.9°F (57.7°C).

Lions live on the tropical grasslands in Africa.

31

The Sun shines all
night in summer at the poles.

Cold climates

The regions surrounding the north
and south poles are the coldest
places on Earth. The Sun's
rays have little warmth there.
Most land in the polar regions
is covered by a thick layer of
ice and snow.

Midnight sun

In summer, each pole tilts toward
the Sun. At night, the Sun dips
low in the sky, but never sets.
So it stays light, even at
midnight. In winter, the
pole leans away from
the Sun. The Sun
never fully rises,
so it is dark all
the time.

Shimmering lights

Swirling curtains of light
sometimes shimmer in the night
sky at the poles. These beautiful
lights are called auroras.
The lights may be red, green,
or purple. This amazing display
is caused by particles from the
Sun hitting gases high in the air.

The Arctic

The area around the North Pole is called the Arctic. This region is mainly an ice-covered ocean. Polar bears and seals live in the sea and on the ice.

This polar bear is hunting seals on the ice.

Penguins have thick feathers and a warm, fatty layer under their skin.

Antarctica

The area around the South Pole is called the Antarctic. The vast icy land of Antarctica lies in this area. Antarctica is covered with a thick cap of ice up to about 1¾ miles (3 km) deep. Penguins and seals live only on the coast.

Rocks and soil

This chapter explains how rocks form and how the rocks at the surface are broken down by rain, wind, frost, and sunlight. Underground, there are many riches, such as gold, silver, and diamonds. Valuable fossil fuels—coal, oil, and gas—come from beneath the ground, too. However, soil, which lies on top of Earth's rocky surface, may be the greatest treasure of all. Read on to find out why.

Rocky planet

We live on Earth's hard, rocky surface called the crust. Deep below the crust, the rocks are hot—so hot they are melted and flow like sticky molasses.

Inside Earth

Scientists believe Earth is made of several layers. The surface crust is thin, like the shell of an egg. Below the crust is a thick layer called the mantle, with red-hot rocks. In the core at the center, the rocks are even hotter.

Inner core

Outer core

Mantle

Crust

Cross section through Earth

Earth's rocky crust at the Grand Canyon

Heat from below

Deep mines are hot because of the hot rocks below. But even the very deepest mines are just like a pinprick in the giant rocky ball that is Earth.

This man is working in a hot, deep mine.

Thin crust

Ocean

Land

Thick crust

Rocky crust

Cliffs and mountains are formed from Earth's crust. If you stripped away the grass, soil, or concrete at any place on Earth, you'd hit rock. These cliffs were made by a river cutting through the rock.

Ocean crust

Earth's crust is thicker beneath the land than beneath the oceans. The crust beneath the land is 12½ to 56 miles (20 to 90 km) thick. Beneath the oceans, it is only about 4½ miles (7 km) thick.

DID YOU KNOW? Scientists believe the temperature at the center of Earth is more than 9,000°F (5,000°C). The outer core is made of partly liquid rock. The inner core is a solid ball of metal.

37

Fiery rocks

Rocks form in different ways. Fiery rocks come from deep underground. Red-hot, liquid rock bubbles up to near the surface, then cools to form solid rock.

Glowing lava

Red-hot, liquid rock deep underground is called magma. When it spills onto the surface at a volcano (see pages 64–75), it is called lava. Lava cools and hardens quickly at the surface.

Frothy pumice

A type of rock called pumice was once frothy lava. Like froth on a soft drink, it contains air bubbles. The bubbles were trapped when the lava cooled. Bubbles make this rock so light it floats on water.

People use pumice to rub away hard skin while bathing.

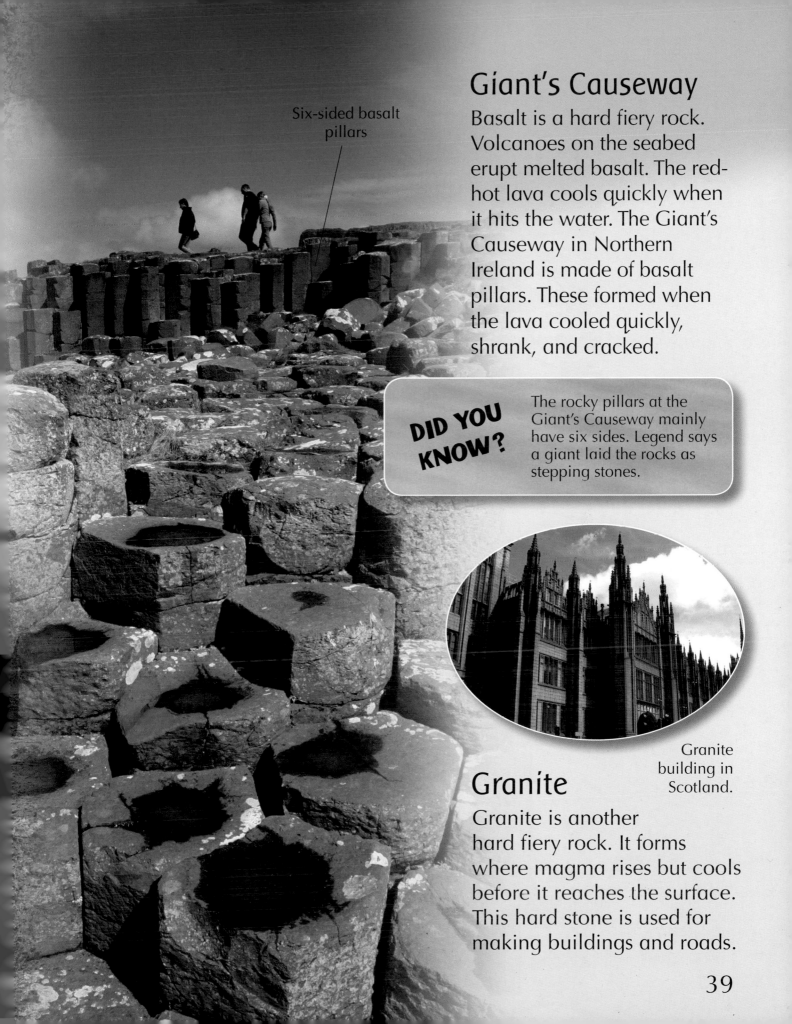

Six-sided basalt pillars

Giant's Causeway

Basalt is a hard fiery rock. Volcanoes on the seabed erupt melted basalt. The red-hot lava cools quickly when it hits the water. The Giant's Causeway in Northern Ireland is made of basalt pillars. These formed when the lava cooled quickly, shrank, and cracked.

DID YOU KNOW?

The rocky pillars at the Giant's Causeway mainly have six sides. Legend says a giant laid the rocks as stepping stones.

Granite building in Scotland.

Granite

Granite is another hard fiery rock. It forms where magma rises but cools before it reaches the surface. This hard stone is used for making buildings and roads.

39

Wearing away

The rocks at the surface are battered by rain, wind, frost, and sunshine. Parts of rock flake off and are carried away by wind and water. This process is called erosion.

This flat slab of limestone is crisscrossed with deep grooves.

Eating into rock

Rainwater contains a weak acid that eats into soft rocks, such as limestone. This is similar to when an aspirin dissolves in water. The rainwater slowly wears deep grooves in the rock.

Shattered by ice

In cold places, such as on mountainsides, water seeps into cracks in the rock and freezes at night. Ice takes up more space than water, so the ice widens the cracks. Eventually, the rock flakes away.

Ice has made this rock crack.

Worn by wind

In dry, windy places, sand and grit are carried on the wind. When the wind blasts against rock, the sand and grit act like sandpaper. This can carve smooth curves into the rock.

This rock in Western Australia is called Wave Rock.

Carried away

When it rains, trickling water carries away small pieces of loose rock. The water drains into streams and rivers, which carry the rocky pieces downhill. They end up in seas or lakes.

Settled rocks

Fiery rocks are not the only type of rock. Another type forms from rocky pieces that are carried out to sea by rivers. The pieces get squashed together by more rocky fragments and eventually turn into solid rock.

Rock layers

When the rocky pieces are carried out to sea, they settle in layers on the seabed. Later, the rock layers may be pushed upward when mountains form (see pages 90–91) and become part of the land.

You can see the rock layers in this sandstone cliff in New Zealand.

Clay pots

Clay is a rock that is soft when wet. Potters shape clay to make pots. The pots are baked in an oven to make them hard.

These children are helping to make a clay pot.

Pudding stone

A rock called conglomerate contains round pebbles that settled on the seabed. When the layer was squashed, the pebbles stuck together. Conglomerate, also called pudding stone, can be made up of large rocks as well as pebbles.

These cliffs are made of chalk.

Chalk

Chalk is a soft, white rock made of the tiny shells of millions of sea creatures. The shells built up on the seabed and were later buried. The shelly layer very slowly turned to chalk. This rock can be used to draw on blackboards and paved areas.

45

Changed rock

Changed rocks are another type of rock. They form when rocks are heated or squeezed below ground. The rocks may be squeezed by other rocks on top of them, or they may be squeezed by magma rising upward, which can also heat the rock.

DID YOU KNOW?

Marble is a changed rock. Some of the world's most famous sculptures have been carved from this rock.

Heated rock

This is a changed rock called gneiss. The wavy lines show where the rock layers have been melted and squeezed. Sometimes squeezing happens when rocks shift underground during earthquakes (see pages 76–85).

Slate

Slate forms when a rock called shale is squashed deep below ground. Slate naturally splits into thin sheets that make great roof tiles.

Marble

Marble forms when limestone rock is heated underground. Heating and squeezing make the rock change color and texture. Marble can be carved easily and its surface polished until it shines.

The Taj Mahal

The Taj Mahal is a beautiful palace in northern India. It is made of white marble and decorated with colored marble. Marble comes in several colors—black, pink, green, and white. Some marble has swirling patterns.

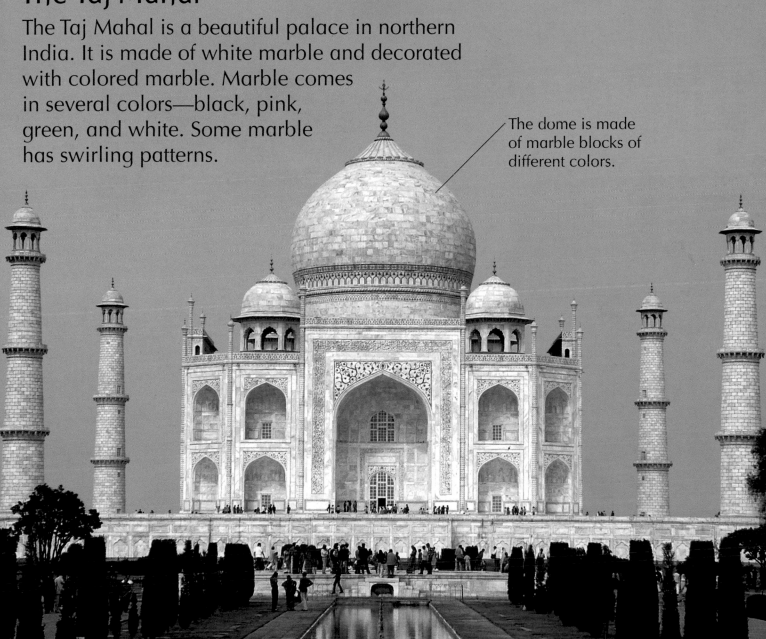

The dome is made of marble blocks of different colors.

Bryce Canyon

Bryce Canyon is a national park in the western United States. It is formed of layered rocks called sandstone, limestone, and mudstone. Over time, water, ice, and wind have carved fantastic shapes into the rocks.

Wildlife park

Animals, such as deer and foxes, live in Bryce Canyon. Some use the rocks for shelter. There are also birds, such as swallows, ravens, and eagles.

Hoodoos

The tall rock spires of Bryce Canyon are called hoodoos. These rocky pillars are made of soft mudstone topped with harder limestone. Ice and water wear the soft mudstone away more quickly than the harder cap of rock.

Water, ice, and wind wear grooves in the rock.

Bryce Canyon facts

- The rocks of Bryce Canyon formed on the beds of lakes and rivers. Over time, the forces that build mountains lifted the rocks 8,200 feet (2,500 m) above sea level.

- Bryce Canyon has more hoodoos than almost any place on the earth.

A bald eagle's wings can measure 8 feet (2.5 m) across.

Colorful rocks

The rocks of Bryce Canyon are pink and orange. The minerals iron and manganese give the rocks their color. At sunrise and sunset, the rocks glow bright red.

Rock arch

Thunderstorms and hailstorms can strike Bryce Canyon in summer. Snow and ice cover the ground in winter. Rain, hail, snow, and ice wear away the rocks to make amazing features, such as this arch below.

DID YOU KNOW?

Bryce Canyon became a national park in 1928. The park covers about 56 square miles (145 sq km). The hoodoos of Bryce Canyon are up to 197 feet (60 m) tall.

Minerals

Rocks are made of natural materials called minerals. There are thousands of different minerals but only about a hundred are common.

Feldspar

Mica

Quartz

Granite

Granite is made up of three different minerals—quartz, mica, and feldspar. They can be seen in this close-up photograph. Granite is used as building stone.

Plaster from gypsum

If you break an arm or a leg, the doctor will put a plaster cast on it while it heals. Plaster is made of a soft mineral called gypsum. The wet plaster sets to make a hard cast.

Wet plaster is molded around the leg.

DID YOU KNOW?

The soft mineral graphite is used to make the lead in pencils. Crayons and paints can be made using another soft mineral called talc.

Copper mines

Valuable minerals, such as copper, are dug from mines. Many mines run deep below ground, but copper is often found near the surface. Copper is used to make water pipes and electrical wire.

Fireworks

Fireworks, such as sparklers, are made from a yellow mineral called sulfur. Sulfur is also used to make matches and explosives. Next time you see a firework display, remember sulfur!

49

Metals

Strong, shiny metals can be worked into different shapes. Metals are found in rocks called ores, often mixed with other minerals. Rare metals, such as gold, are expensive.

Lump of gold ore

Gold wedding ring

DID YOU KNOW?

The largest gold nugget ever found weighed 154 pounds (70 kg). It was found in Victoria, Australia, in 1869. The lump was nicknamed the Welcome Stranger!

Gold

Gold is usually found in rocks deep below ground. But a few lucky people have found whole lumps, called nuggets, at the surface! Specks of gold are sometimes washed out of rocks by water, and are found on riverbeds.

Silver

Silver is another rare metal found in an ore. Ores are usually crushed and heated to get the metal out. Silver is sometimes used to make coins.

These silver coins come from ancient Greece.

50

Gold rush

When someone discovers gold, thousands of people rush to the same area, hoping to get rich. This is called a gold rush. Gold in river gravel is collected by swirling the gravel around in a pan. The gold sinks to the bottom. This is called panning.

A miner panning for gold in California in 1890.

Making iron

Iron is made by heating iron ore in a hot furnace. Limestone and coke (a type of coal) are also added. Hot, liquid iron runs out at the bottom of the furnace. Iron is used to make an even stronger metal called steel.

Red-hot, runny iron flows from the furnace into a container.

Gems and jewels

Minerals called gemstones are made into jewels. Experts cut and polish the stones until they sparkle. There are more than 50 different kinds of gemstones. They are all rare, but some are very rare.

Uncut diamond

Rough diamond

A diamond forms when a material called carbon is heated and squeezed very hard underground. Diamonds do not have much sparkle when they come out of the ground. Many sides are cut into the stone to make it sparkle.

DID YOU KNOW? Diamonds are the hardest mineral found on Earth. They are used to make cutting tools as well as jewels.

This diamond has been cut and polished so it sparkles.

Crystals

Most gemstones form as even-sided crystals. Each type of crystal has a regular shape with a certain number of sides. You can see the large, purple crystals in this chunk of amethyst.

Many colors

Gemstones come in many beautiful colors. Sapphires are blue, emeralds are bright green, and rubies and garnets are dark red. Opals have many colors. They are not cut with many sides but are smoothed and rounded.

Most large opals come from Australia.

Crown jewels

The crown of the British king or queen has more than 3,000 jewels! One of the largest stones is a famous diamond called the Cullinan II Diamond. The largest red stone is called the Black Prince's Ruby.

Fossil fuels

Most of the energy we use at home comes from coal, oil, and gas. They are formed from fossils—the remains of prehistoric plants and animals. That's why we call them fossil fuels.

A lump of coal

Coal mining

Coal is usually found deep below ground in layers called seams. A deep hole called a shaft is dug to reach the coal. Coal is burned in power stations to produce electricity for homes and factories.

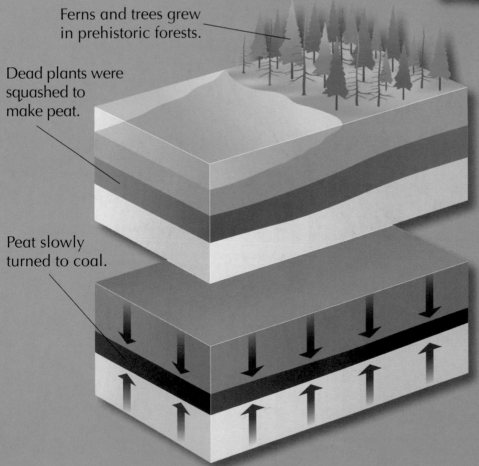

Ferns and trees grew in prehistoric forests.

Dead plants were squashed to make peat.

Peat slowly turned to coal.

How coal was made

Coal formed when prehistoric plants from swampy forests died and sank into the swamp. They were squashed as soil and rock built up on top and slowly hardened into peat, a type of soil. The peat then slowly hardened into coal.

54

Oil and gas

Oil and gas are the remains of tiny sea creatures that were buried and squashed on the seabed. They slowly turned to oil and gas. These fuels are mined from the seabed by drilling deep holes. Oil is made into fuel for cars. Gas is used for cooking and heating.

Cars burn fuel to power their engines.

DID YOU KNOW?

When cars, factories, and power stations burn fossil fuels, they give off waste gases that cause pollution. The pollution is making the world's climate warmer. Find out more about this on pages 212–213.

Made from oil

Oil has many uses. Plastic and nylon are made from the leftovers when oil is purified. Paint, lipstick, and candles are also made from oil.

All these plastic objects are made from oil.

Soil story

You may not think of soil as valuable. But in a way, soil is even more precious than gold, oil, or diamonds. Plants need soil to grow, and animals need plants for food. So most living things depend on soil.

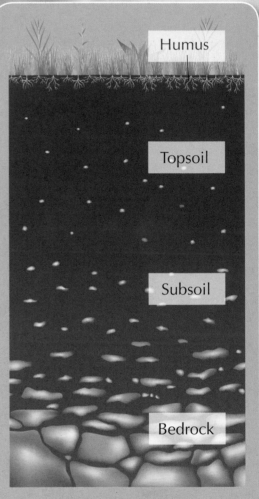

Humus

Topsoil

Subsoil

Bedrock

Soil layers

Soil contains several layers. At the very top is a thin layer of rotting plants called humus. The rich topsoil contains plant and animal remains. The subsoil below contains broken rocks. At the bottom is solid bedrock.

How soil is made

Soil is made from tiny parts of rock mixed with plant and animal remains. Soil begins to form as ice, water, and wind break rocks into pieces. Plants take root in the rocky pieces. Rotting plants and animal remains make the soil richer.

Tree roots

Trees spread their roots through the soil. The roots draw water and nourishing minerals from the soil. They also anchor the tree in windy weather. Roots break up rocks to form more soil.

Different soils

There are many types of soil. Sandy and chalky soils are dry and powdery. Clay soil is sticky. Different plants like different types of soil. Gardeners need to choose the right plants for the soil in their garden.

DID YOU KNOW?

It takes hundreds of years to form even a thin layer of soil. Soil is much deeper in some places than others—it may be anything from a few inches to several feet deep.

Life in soil

Soil contains thousands of different living things, from tiny insects and spiders to earthworms and larger animals, such as moles and rabbits. The crops that provide our food grow in soil.

Animal burrows

Earthworms and moles burrow in the soil. Their tunnels let air and water in. This helps to make the soil more fertile. Worms and moles spend their lives under the ground.

Eat and be eaten

Living things in the soil depend on one another for food. Earthworms feed on rotting leaves. Moles feed on earthworms. When animals die, their remains nourish the soil, which helps more plants to grow.

The violent Earth

Volcanoes and earthquakes are two of nature's scariest wonders. Rivers of hot, melted rock gush from an erupting volcano. Ash, rocks, and gas blast high in the air. During an earthquake, the ground heaves and houses, trees, and bridges collapse. Earthquakes and volcanoes happen because of powerful forces underground. Read on to find out when, where, and why earthquakes strike and volcanoes erupt.

Earth's crust

Earth's hard outer crust sits on top of red-hot, squishy rock. The crust is not one solid layer but is made of giant slabs of rock. The huge slabs are called plates.

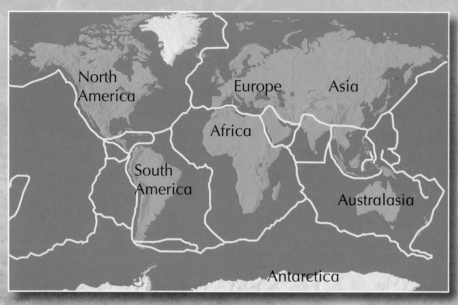

These yellow lines show the edges of Earth's plates.

Moving plates

Earth's plates fit together like pieces in an enormous jigsaw puzzle. Currents in the melted rock below cause the plates to drift very slowly. These movements produce earthquakes and volcanoes on Earth's surface.

Faults

As Earth's plates move very slowly across the surface, they bump and scrape one another. Where two plates scrape together, a long crack called a fault sometimes appears.

A fault at the point where two plates meet in Iceland.

Volcanoes

Earth's crust is thin and weak where the plates meet. Red-hot, melted rock wells up from below, breaks through, and spills out onto the surface. We call these places volcanoes (see pages 64–75).

Earthquakes

Plates moving past each other sometimes jolt violently. The jolt, which makes the ground shake, is called an earthquake (see pages 76–85). Earthquakes can do great damage.

An earthquake has made this building in Japan collapse.

DID YOU KNOW?

Earth's plates move very, very slowly. They shift about 1 inch (2.5 cm) each year. People's fingernails grow at about the same rate.

Volcanic eruptions

When melted rock known as lava spills out of a volcano, it is called an eruption. Lava rushes out in fiery rivers, then cools to form solid rock. It slowly builds up in layers to form a mountain.

Inside a volcano

Red-hot rock inside Earth is called magma. Magma builds up below the volcano in a magma chamber. As more magma rises, the pressure builds up. Red-hot lava, ash, gas, and steam burst out through the top of the volcano.

Ash

Crater

Magma

Magma chamber

Flying rocks

Some volcanoes shoot chunks of red-hot rocks high in the air. The hot rocks fly through the air and then splatter on the ground. These deadly rocks are called lava bombs.

Lava shoots out of the crater of a volcano in Hawaii.

Hollow crater

The opening in the top of the volcano is called the crater. As the eruption dies down, the large hole is blocked by ash and solid lava. These shoot out with great force the next time the volcano erupts.

 Lava

Glowing clouds

During some eruptions, clouds of burning ash pour out of the volcano. These heavy clouds spill down the mountain, moving much faster than lava. They burn anything in their path.

A huge cloud of ash erupts from Mount Mayon, a volcano in the Philippines.

Types of volcano

The shape of a volcano depends on the type of lava that spills out of it. The two main types of volcanoes are tall, cone-shaped volcanoes and flatter shield volcanoes.

Underwater volcanoes

Some volcanoes erupt under the sea. The hot lava cools as soon as it hits the water. This forms rounded lumps of rock called pillow lava.

Cone-shaped volcanoes

Some volcanoes explode violently, throwing out thick, sticky lava. This type of lava flows only a short way before cooling and turning solid. Layers of lava and ash build up to form a cone-shaped mountain.

A cone-shaped volcano in the Philippines.

A shield volcano on the islands of Hawaii.

Shield volcanoes

Some volcanoes erupt runny lava. This lava flows a long way before cooling and turning solid. A low, rounded hill called a shield volcano eventually forms.

Snow covers the top of a dormant volcano in Africa.

Sleeping volcano

Not all volcanoes erupt all the time. A volcano that has not erupted for a long time but may erupt again is called a dormant volcano. "Dormant" means "sleeping." A volcano that has stopped erupting is called an extinct volcano.

DID YOU KNOW?

Volcanoes that have erupted recently, or are still erupting, are called active volcanoes. There are more than 1,000 active volcanoes around the world, but only 20 to 30 actually erupt each year.

67

Mount St. Helens

In May 1980, a volcano called Mount St. Helens in Washington suddenly erupted. The whole top of the mountain blew off in a violent explosion.

Before the eruption

Mount St. Helens had not erupted for 123 years before the 1980 eruption. The mountain looked peaceful, but inside the pressure was slowly building.

Whoosh!

When Mount St. Helens erupted, ash, gas, and steam escaped with an enormous "whoosh." People living hundreds of miles away heard the explosion. A thick layer of ash rained down on the countryside.

Wrecked forests

Forests of tall trees covered the lower slopes of Mount St. Helens before the eruption. The blast snapped the trees like matchsticks.

Eruption facts

🌍 The cloud of ash from Mount St. Helens rose 12½ miles (20 km) in the sky. The ash made the sky dark and drifted on the wind to settle over a wide area. Towns up to 185 miles (300 km) away were covered in ash.

🌍 Mount St. Helens erupted violently for four days. Smaller eruptions continued for several months afterward.

New life

After the eruption, Mount St. Helens looked lifeless. Ash lay thick on the ground and choked lakes and rivers. But after just a few months, plants began to sprout and animals returned to Mount St. Helens.

Famous eruptions

The most powerful eruptions do a lot of damage. When water or snow mixes with volcanic ash, it produces a tide of mud, which can destroy towns and villages.

A model of a dog made by pouring plaster into a hollow in the ash.

Mount Vesuvius

About 2,000 years ago, a volcano called Vesuvius erupted in southern Italy. The Roman town of Pompeii was buried under a thick layer of ash and was not discovered again for hundreds of years.

Buried by ash

When hot ash rained down on Pompeii, many people died. The bodies of some people and animals left behind hollow spaces in the hard ash.

Deadly ash

In 1991, Mount Pinatubo on the Philippines erupted, and ash covered the landscape. Heavy rain turned the ash to mud, which swept across the island. Several villages were buried by the mud.

Tide of mud

In 1985, the Nevado del Ruiz volcano high in the Andes Mountains in South America erupted. Red-hot lava and ash melted snow on the mountain. A tide of mud roared downhill and buried the town of Armero in the valley below.

71

Volcanic wonders

The heat from volcanoes creates amazing volcanic landscapes, which include hot springs and mud pools. The soil around volcanoes also makes good land for growing crops.

Hot springs

In hot springs, the water is heated by hot rocks underground. People like to bathe in the warm water. Some monkeys in Japan bathe in hot volcanic springs to keep warm during the icy winter.

Monkeys at the hot springs in Nagano, Japan.

Useful volcanoes

Volcanic rock and ash break down to make rich soil for farming. This farmland is on the slopes of a volcano in the Philippines. Coconut trees and rice grow well in the fertile volcanic soil.

Steam from this geyser erupts high into the air.

Bubbling mud

In some volcanic areas, water mixes with hot ash to make pools of bubbling mud. The mud is rich in minerals. Some people put volcanic mud on their faces and bodies because they believe it is good for their skin.

Hot fountain

Water trickling underground may be heated by hot rocks. When the water reaches boiling point, it shoots upward, like steam from a steam train. The fountain of hot water is called a geyser.

73

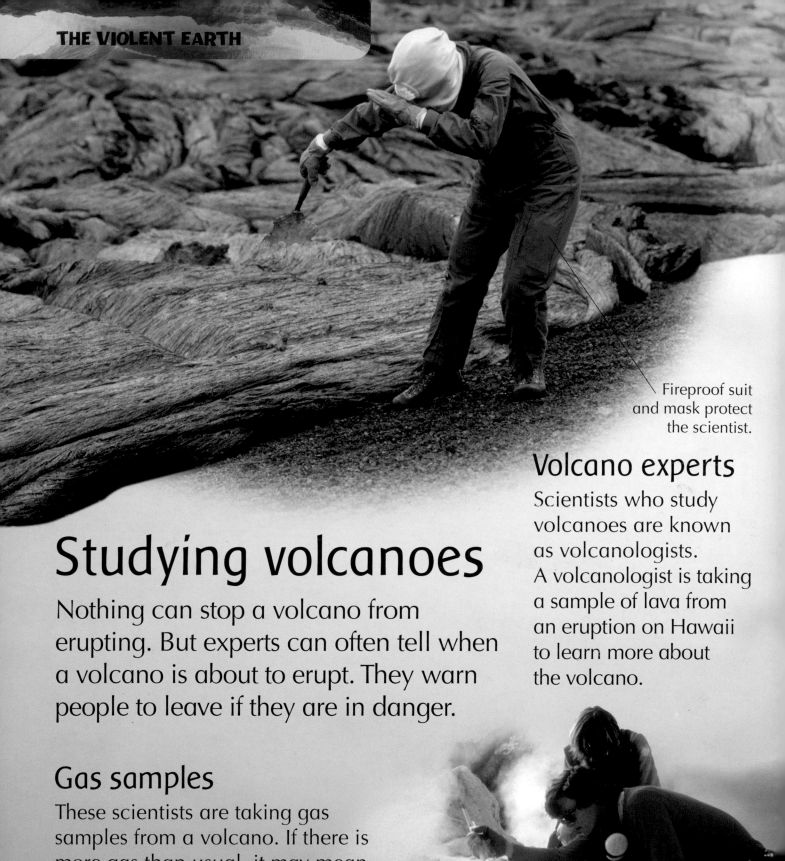

Fireproof suit
and mask protect
the scientist.

Volcano experts

Scientists who study
volcanoes are known
as volcanologists.
A volcanologist is taking
a sample of lava from
an eruption on Hawaii
to learn more about
the volcano.

Studying volcanoes

Nothing can stop a volcano from
erupting. But experts can often tell when
a volcano is about to erupt. They warn
people to leave if they are in danger.

Gas samples

These scientists are taking gas
samples from a volcano. If there is
more gas than usual, it may mean
that the volcano is about to erupt.
One volcanic gas, sulfur dioxide,
smells like rotten eggs.

Time to go

When people have to leave because a volcano is about to erupt, it is called an evacuation. These people are evacuating the island of Montserrat in the Caribbean because of danger from a nearby volcano.

Keeping watch

If an eruption is about to happen, gas and steam may start to leak from a volcano. The mountain may bulge as melted rock builds up inside. The scientist, below, is checking the shape of Mount St. Helens in 2004 to make sure it is still safe.

DID YOU KNOW?

Some volcanoes still fool the experts by erupting without warning. In 1973, a volcano in Iceland suddenly started to spout red-hot lava. Everyone had thought the volcano was extinct!

This huge crater was made by the 1980 eruption.

Earthquakes

The plates that form Earth's crust are always moving slowly. This puts the rocks below ground under great strain. An earthquake happens when the rocks suddenly jolt into a new position.

Shock waves

Earthquakes usually start deep underground. The point where rocks grind and shatter is called the focus. Shock waves spread out in all directions. The damage is worst on the surface directly above.

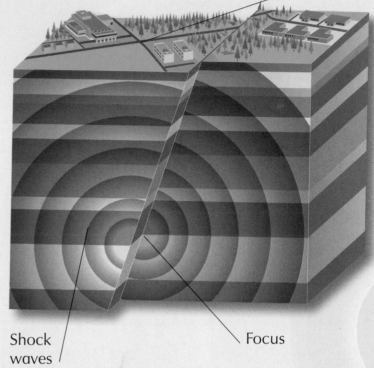

Epicenter is the point on the surface directly above the focus.

Shock waves

Focus

Wrecked buildings

Powerful earthquakes make the ground shake. Buildings can be torn from their foundations. Glass shatters and steel beams bend like rubber. Houses sway and crash to the ground.

DID YOU KNOW?

Thousands of earthquakes strike each year, but most are tiny. Small quakes make lightbulbs swing and ornaments rattle. The most powerful earthquakes wreck whole towns.

Cracked ground

When an earthquake strikes, the violent shaking can make the ground split open. Huge cracks can appear in roads and sidewalks. Some cracks are big enough to swallow cars!

Broken bridge

Strong earthquakes can damage roads and bridges. In 1995, an earthquake in Japan destroyed this highway. Wrecked roads and railroads can make it difficult for outside help to reach a region hit by an earthquake.

This crack appeared in a road after an earthquake in California in 1989.

77

Effects of earthquakes

An earthquake lasts only a few seconds, but the shaking can do terrible damage. Earthquakes also start fires, cause landslides, and turn solid ground to mud.

Fire!

Fires start when gas pipes and electricity lines are damaged by earthquakes. In 1989, fire swept through San Francisco, California, after an earthquake. Water pipes were damaged by the earthquake, making it difficult for firefighters to put out the flames.

Dam burst

Powerful earthquakes can destroy dams built on rivers. A wall of water then bursts through the dam and rushes downriver. Towns and villages lower down are swept away. This dam in Taiwan was wrecked by an earthquake in 1989.

The landslide started on this hillside.

Landslide

When the ground shakes, loose soil and rock can slip away in a landslide. This landslide happened after a quake in Central America in 2001.

Sinking ground

Violent shaking can turn clay or sandy soil to mud. Buildings sink into the mud or topple over. These buildings collapsed after an earthquake hit Niigata, Japan, in 1964.

Tsunamis

Earthquakes can strike under the sea as well as on land. When an earthquake shakes the seabed, it can cause powerful waves called tsunamis. These waves race across the ocean and wreck towns when they reach the coast.

2004 tsunami

In December 2004, a powerful earthquake rocked the seabed off Indonesia in Southeast Asia. Strong waves spread out like ripples. The waves traveled 3,100 miles (5,000 km) to wreck towns on the shores of India and even Africa.

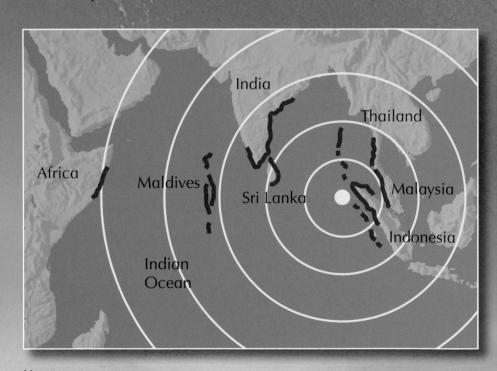

Key to map

— Areas hit by the tsunami

● Epicentre

◎ Waves spreading outwards

All the buildings in this town in Indonesia were destroyed by the 2004 tsunami.

Krakatoa

Volcanic eruptions can also cause tsunamis. In 1883, a volcano on an island called Krakatoa, near Indonesia, exploded.

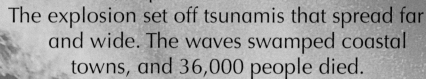

The explosion set off tsunamis that spread far and wide. The waves swamped coastal towns, and 36,000 people died.

Towering waves

Out at sea, tsunamis form low waves that aren't very noticeable. But they build up to become much taller when they reach shallow water. The huge waves are a terrifying sight when they smash onto the shore.

Wrecked coast

Damage from the 2004 tsunami was worst on the coast of Indonesia. Whole towns were completely flattened by the waves. Boats were swept onto the shore and carried far inland.

Deadly earthquakes

Earthquakes can be incredibly destructive. The damage is often worst in cities, where many people are killed by falling buildings. Earthquakes have brought disaster to many parts of the world.

DID YOU KNOW?

San Francisco lies on a fault where two plates scrape past each other. This fault runs for about 750 miles (1,200 km) along the western coast of the United States. Earthquakes strike San Francisco often—in 1906, 1989, and 1994.

Lisbon, 1755

In 1755, an earthquake struck out at sea near the city of Lisbon in Portugal. Huge waves wrecked Lisbon's harbor. Candles burning in churches and houses were knocked over and fires started all over the city.

San Francisco, 1906

In 1906, a powerful earthquake wrecked the city of San Francisco in California. Fires broke out and raged for days because firefighters ran out of water.

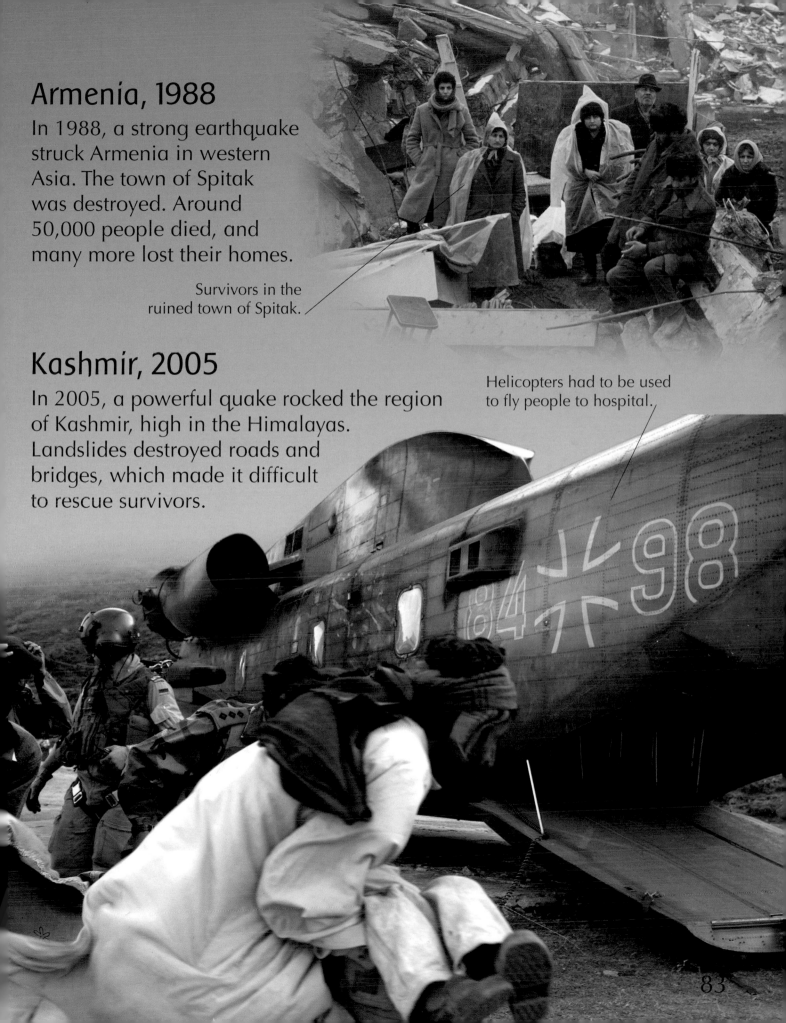

Armenia, 1988

In 1988, a strong earthquake struck Armenia in western Asia. The town of Spitak was destroyed. Around 50,000 people died, and many more lost their homes.

Survivors in the ruined town of Spitak.

Kashmir, 2005

In 2005, a powerful quake rocked the region of Kashmir, high in the Himalayas. Landslides destroyed roads and bridges, which made it difficult to rescue survivors.

Helicopters had to be used to fly people to hospital.

Watching earthquakes

Scientists use machines to measure the strength of earthquakes. If experts believe an earthquake is due, they warn everyone. But it is very hard to say exactly when and where an earthquake will strike.

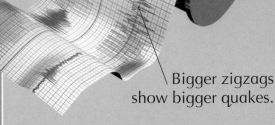

Bigger zigzags show bigger quakes.

In 1975, scientists in the Chinese city of Haicheng noticed animals acting strangely. They ordered everyone to leave the city. A few hours later an earthquake struck.

Measuring quakes

A seismograph measures the shaking caused by earthquakes. Pens attached to weights hang above a roll of paper. When an earthquake strikes, the paper shakes, and the pens draw zigzags on the paper.

Animal warnings

Animals often act strangely just before an earthquake. Rats run away, while cats meow and dogs bark. Some experts believe that animals can hear the very high, faint noises made by rocks that are stretched to breaking point before a quake.

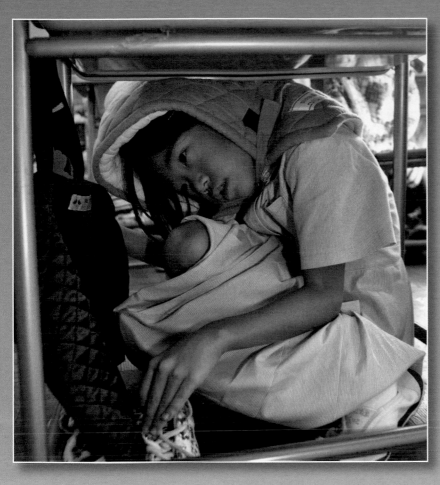

The pyramid shape of this building helps it stay upright in an earthquake.

Safety practice

If an earthquake strikes, people should stay indoors and hide under a strong desk or table. This Japanese child is practicing what to do in an earthquake. She is wearing a padded hood to protect her head.

Safer buildings

In areas where earthquakes are likely, people design buildings that will cope with the shaking. This tall building in San Francisco has strong steel beams to support it.

Mountains and glaciers

Mountains are the highest places on the earth. This chapter explains how these rocky peaks form and describes some of the plants and animals that live there. Read on to find out about mountain dangers and about living in and visiting these high places. This chapter also explains what glaciers are and how they form.

Snow-covered K2
is 28,251 feet
(8,611 m) tall.

Towering mountains

Mountains are high, rocky areas that rise above their surroundings. Many mountains have steep, sloping sides, and the tops of very high mountains are cold and covered with snow.

Mountain chains

Some mountains stand alone, but many form long lines called chains or are found in groups called ranges. The Andes in South America is the longest mountain chain on land, stretching for 4,475 miles (7,200 km).

South America

Andes

88

Mauna Kea

Sea level

Mauna Kea is 33,480 feet (10,205 m) from the seabed.

Pacific Ocean

Seabed

Rising from the ocean

Mountains are measured from sea level. Mauna Kea, a mountain in Hawaii, rises 13,795 feet (4,205 m) above the surface of the sea, but the rest of the peak lies underwater. Mauna Kea is taller than Mount Everest when measured from the seabed.

The Himalayas

The Himalayas in southern Asia are the world's highest mountains. This range includes Mount Everest. At 29,078 feet (8,863 m), it is Earth's highest mountain on land.

Africa's highest peak

Mount Kilimanjaro is the tallest peak in Africa. This mountain rises to 19,340 feet (5,895 m). The top is covered with snow, although Kilimanjaro is near the equator, where the climate is hot.

Fold mountains

Many of the world's highest mountains are found in places where two plates of Earth's crust push against each other. Rocks are pushed upward, forming fold mountains.

Fold mountains in the Pyrenees in Spain.

How fold mountains form

Fold mountain ranges form where two of Earth's plates crash together. The land in between the plates is pushed up and the rocks fold, forming mountain peaks. The Himalayas in Asia, and the Pyrenees and Alps in Europe, are fold mountain ranges.

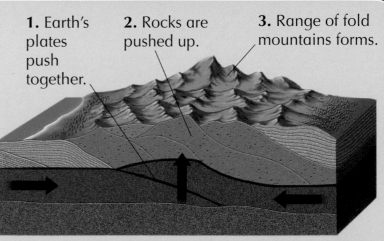

1. Earth's plates push together.

2. Rocks are pushed up.

3. Range of fold mountains forms.

Zigzag rocks

As the layers of this rock in Great Britain were squashed, they folded to form these amazing zigzag patterns.

Volcanic mountains

Volcanoes are another type of mountain. These form when hot, melted rock erupts on Earth's surface. Layers of erupted rock build up to make tall, cone-shaped mountains.

Cotopaxi is a volcanic mountain in Ecuador, South America.

91

Blocks and domes

Two other types of mountains are steep-sided block mountains and rounded dome mountains. All mountains take millions of years to form, but some are much older than others. Young mountains are usually much higher than old mountains.

The Tetons in North America are block mountains.

Block mountains

The movement of Earth's plates sometimes causes long cracks called faults to appear (see page 62). If a huge slab of rock is pushed upward between two faults, it makes a steep-sided peak called a block mountain.

How block mountains form

This diagram shows how blocks of rock are pushed upward between faults to form mountains. If a block of land slips down between faults, it forms a deep, flattish valley. This is called a rift valley.

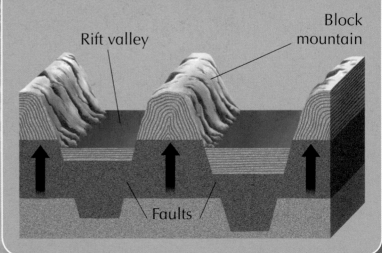

Rift valley

Block mountain

Faults

How dome mountains form

Dome mountains form where hot, melted rock pushes up but cools before it reaches the surface. The layered rocks on top are pushed up into a dome shape. Later, the rocks on top wear away to reveal the dome of volcanic rock.

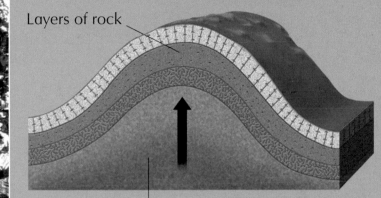

Layers of rock

Dome of volcanic rock

DID YOU KNOW?

Ben Nevis, the highest peak in Great Britain, is 4,406 feet (1,343 m) tall and is part of the Grampians range in Scotland. The range was once as high as the Himalayas, but has worn down over millions of years.

Worn smooth

Mountains are slowly worn away by the weather. Over millions of years, high, jagged mountains become lower and smoother. Ben Nevis (left) in Scotland is a very old dome mountain with a rounded top.

Mount Everest

At 29,078 feet (8,863 m) tall, Mount Everest is the world's highest mountain. This famous peak lies in the Himalayas, on the border between Nepal and Tibet in China. The mountain's local name, Chomolungma, means "mother goddess of the world."

Snow covers the bare, rocky slopes of Mount Everest.

DID YOU KNOW?

Lhotse, the world's fourth-highest mountain, lies very close to Everest. The two mountains are linked by a snowy ridge.

Climbing Everest

The first climbers to reach the top of Everest were Edmund Hillary from New Zealand and Tenzing Norgay from Nepal in 1953. Since then, many others have climbed the mountain, although it is difficult and dangerous.

Mount Everest facts

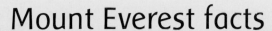

- The height of Everest was first measured by surveyors in the 1800s. They named it after Sir George Everest, a famous British surveyor.
- Italian Reinhold Messner was the first person to climb Everest alone and without using bottled oxygen to help him breathe.
- More than 2,000 people have reached the top of Everest.

Sherpas

Sherpas are mountain people that live in the Everest region in Nepal. These people are used to the cold and are very fit. Some work as mountain guides and others carry loads up the steep slopes.

Sherpas balance heavy loads on their backs.

Sherpa town

Namche Bazaar is the biggest village near Everest. Sherpas live there. Not long ago the village was tiny, but now climbers and walkers stay there on their way to Everest. Namche Bazaar has become a busy town.

Cliffs and crags

Rain, wind, and ice can carve mountains into amazing shapes, including steep cliffs, uneven craggy rocks, and tall, rocky pillars.

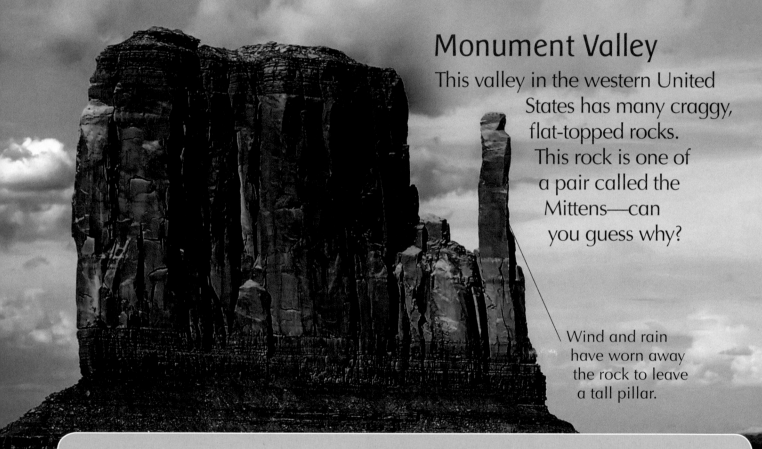

Monument Valley

This valley in the western United States has many craggy, flat-topped rocks. This rock is one of a pair called the Mittens—can you guess why?

Wind and rain have worn away the rock to leave a tall pillar.

Devil's marbles

These amazing rocks are found in the Tanami Desert in Australia. It is very hot there in the day and freezing at night. The heat and the cold make the rocks flake. This has formed rounded shapes that look like giant marbles.

Uluru

This mass of sandstone rock in central Australia is called Uluru. The 1,142-foot (348-m)-tall rock is all that is left of a mountain range that once covered the area.

DID YOU KNOW?

Uluru is also called Ayers Rock. It is a holy place for the Aboriginals, the native people of Australia.

Dartmoor tors

Rocky hills called tors are made of a hard fiery rock called granite. Frost and rain crack the rocks and help form the craggy shapes. Many tors are found on Dartmoor in southern England.

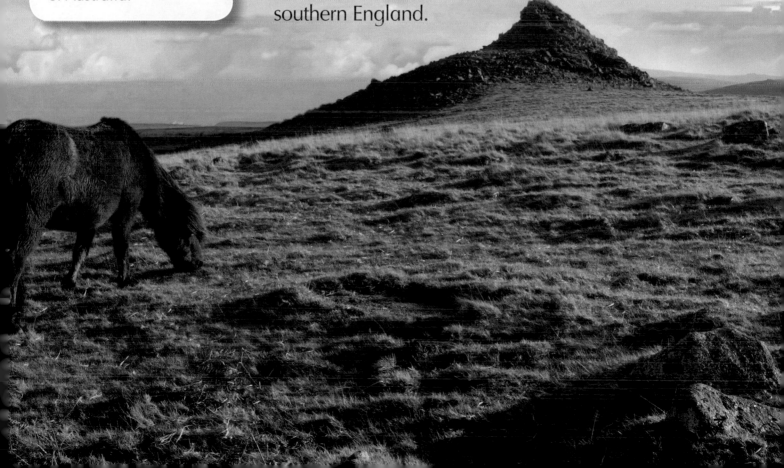

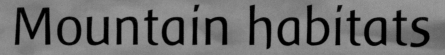

Mountain habitats

Mountains have extreme weather conditions with long, icy winters. The weather is often windy, rainy, or snowy. Mountain plants and animals have to be tough to cope.

Brrrrr!

Mountain air is thinner (contains less gas) than air in the lowlands. Thin air can hold less of the Sun's heat, so the higher up you climb the colder it gets.

People who live on or visit the mountains have to wear warm clothes to keep out the cold.

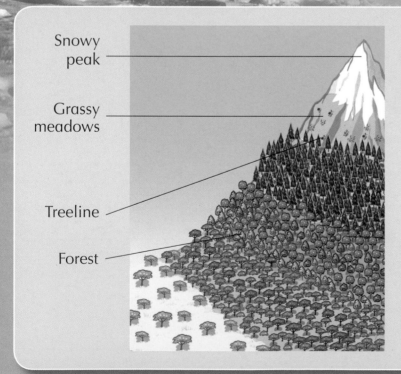

Snowy peak

Grassy meadows

Treeline

Forest

Mountain plants

Different plants grow at different heights on mountains. Trees only grow on lower slopes. At the top, no plants can grow, and snow covers the bare rock. On the middle slopes, there are grassy meadows filled with flowers.

Trees do not grow on mountains above a point called the tree line.

Mountain animals

Animals that live high on mountains have thick hair to keep them warm. Birds have extra-warm feathers. This llama lives in the Andes. Llamas have large lungs that help them breathe the thin mountain air.

DID YOU KNOW?

Animals called marmots live on high mountains in many parts of the world. They stay there all year, spending the winter sleeping in their burrows. This is called hibernation.

Moving up and down

Goatlike animals, called chamois (below), live in the Alps. They move up the mountain to eat grass in summer. In fall, they move down to the valley to shelter there throughout the cold winter.

Rubbery hooves grip the slippery rocks.

Mountain dangers

Living in or visiting mountain regions can be dangerous. Sometimes, extreme weather may cause rocks or snow to break loose and roar down the mountain.

Landslides

In 2005, houses on this hillside in California were swept away by a landslide. Heavy rain caused chunks of rock on the hillside to become loose and fall downhill.

DID YOU KNOW?

People who are not used to being high up on a mountain can get mountain sickness. They may get a headache and feel sick and dizzy. The cure is to go lower down the mountain.

Preventing avalanches

These fences have been built to protect a village in the Alps from avalanches. The fences keep the snow in place. The danger is greatest when deep snow starts to melt in spring.

Avalanche!

An avalanche is when a mass of snow slips down a mountain. Loud noises or even people skiing can set off an avalanche. The snow gathers speed and roars downhill at up to 185 miles (300 km) an hour.

Mountain rescue

If someone is buried by an avalanche, rescuers have to work very quickly. Dogs can be used to sniff out the person. Then rescuers use spades to remove the snow.

Rescue dogs use their good sense of smell to find people buried in avalanches.

Using mountains

People use mountains in many different ways. Farmers grow crops or rear animals on steep hillsides. Miners dig valuable minerals from the rocks. But most mountain regions have few towns because of the harsh conditions.

Farming

Farmers grow crops, such as potatoes and rice, which can cope with the tough conditions. Low walls are built on steep slopes to make flat fields called terraces.

Rice is being grown in terraces on this steep hillside.

Animals

Farmers rear animals, such as sheep, yaks, goats, and llamas, for their meat, milk, and wool. These animals will graze on slopes that are too steep and stony for farming.

Yaks are used to carry heavy loads in the Himalayas.

Mountain village

Most mountain villages are built in sheltered valleys, not on windy mountaintops. But extreme conditions can still make life difficult for mountain people. This village is in the Himalayas region of Nepal.

Mining in mountains

Gold, silver, and copper are found in some mountains. Miners dig deep tunnels, such as this one in a silver mine, to find the rocks that contain the precious metal.

DID YOU KNOW?

El Alto in Bolivia is one of the world's highest towns. It is 13,450 feet (4,100 m) high in the Andes Mountains in South America. La Paz, the capital of Bolivia, is the world's highest capital at 11,810 feet (3,600 m).

103

Visiting the mountains

Some people visit mountains to enjoy the beautiful scenery and amazing wildlife. Others like to climb the steep mountainsides or ski down snow-covered slopes.

Winter sports

Skiing and snowboarding are popular sports in winter. People visit ski resorts, which have safe, snowy slopes and lifts to carry them up the mountain. It takes a lot of practice to become a good skier!

Hiking

Hiking is a great way to see fantastic mountain scenery. Some hikers carry a tent and all their food in a backpack. Others stay in mountain huts. These backpackers are climbing in the Pirin Mountains in Bulgaria.

Transport

Steep slopes make travel difficult in the mountains. Roads run along the valleys or zigzag up to high passes. Cable cars carry people up very steep slopes or from peak to peak.

A cable car to Sugar Loaf Mountain, Brazil.

Watching wildlife

Some people visit mountains to see wildlife, such as birds or butterflies, or flowers in springtime. Parks have been set up in many mountains to protect rare plants and animals, such as the mountain gorillas in Africa.

DID YOU KNOW?

Tunnels have been blasted right through some mountains to build roads and railroads. A tunnel under Mont Blanc, Europe's highest peak, runs for about 7 miles (11.5 km).

Tourists watch a mountain gorilla in Congo, Africa.

Icy glaciers

Glaciers are found in high mountains. They are rivers of ice that move very slowly downhill, scraping off pieces of rock as they flow.

How do glaciers form?

On high mountains, snow does not melt but builds up into a thick layer. The snow underneath gets squashed down and turns to ice. The ice gets so heavy and slippery that it starts to slide downhill.

At the end

At the lowest end of the glacier, the ice begins to melt because the air there is a little warmer. Any pieces of rock carried along in the ice are dumped at the end of the glacier.

Deep cracks form where the ice splits.

The world's longest glacier is the Lambert-Fisher Glacier in Antarctica. It flows for 320 miles (515 km) from the Antarctic Mountains toward the sea.

Oetzi, the ice man

In 1991, two climbers found the remains of a prehistoric man in a glacier in the Alps. The man had died while on a mountain journey about 5,000 years ago. His body had been preserved by the ice. He was named Oetzi, after the valley where he was found.

This is what Oetzi may have looked like.

Joining together

Pieces of rock are carried along the sides of glaciers, forming dark stripes called moraines. When smaller glaciers join together, the stripes meet in the middle— as can be seen in this Swiss glacier (right).

The Aletsch glacier in Switzerland is the longest in Europe.

Worn by glaciers

Glaciers used to cover much more of Earth than today (see pages 110–111). When these glaciers melted, they left scenery shaped by ice, including U-shaped valleys and steep-sided fjords.

DID YOU KNOW?

Most glaciers flow slowly, moving 3–6½ feet (1–2 m) a day. The Quarayaq Glacier in Greenland flows much faster—more than 65 feet (20 m) a day.

Sheer sides

This tall, pointed peak was carved by glaciers flowing down all sides of the mountain. It is called the Matterhorn and is found in the Alps in Switzerland.

U-shaped valleys

As a glacier flows downhill, it acts like a giant bulldozer. The ice gouges out a deep valley with a flat bottom. Rocks and boulders carried along beneath the glacier scrape away more soil and rock.

A glacier carved this deep, U-shaped valley in Wales.

Mountain tarns

Small, round lakes called tarns were carved by glaciers. The ice gouged out bowl-shaped hollows high in mountains. When the ice melted, the hollows filled with water.

A cruise ship visits a steep-sided fjord in Norway.

Fjords

Fjords are steep-sided valleys at the coast. They were carved by glaciers thousands of years ago. Later, the ice melted and the sea rose to flood the valleys, creating fjords.

Ice caps

In very cold places, the snow never melts. Packed-down snow builds up to form a thick layer of ice called an ice cap. In the past, ice covered much more of Earth's surface than it does today.

North America

Arctic ice cap today

Asia

Europe

Australia

Antarctic ice cap today

South America

Africa

Polar ice

Thick ice covers the land at the Arctic and Antarctic (see page 33). In winter, the icy area gets bigger as the sea freezes over. In summer, the sea ice melts, and the icy area shrinks again.

Ice samples, or cores, contain ice from lower layers.

Old ice

The Antarctic ice cap is up to 2½ miles (4 km) deep. The ice at the bottom is made of snow that fell hundreds of years ago. Scientists study the old ice to find out what conditions were like all those years ago.

110

Ice Ages

During long, cold periods called Ice Ages, ice covered much of Europe and North America. This map shows the area covered by ice in the last Ice Age, which ended about 10,000 years ago.

Arctic ice cap 18,000 years ago

Compare this with the map on page 110, showing the Arctic ice cap today.

Compare this with the map on page 110, showing the Arctic ice cap today.

DID YOU KNOW?

Ice covers about a tenth of Earth's surface today. During the last Ice Age, it covered about a fourth of the planet.

Woolly mammoth

Huge, hairy elephants called mammoths lived in Asia, Europe, and North America during the last Ice Age. Bodies of mammoths have been found in the ice in northern Russia. When the Ice Age ended, mammoths died out.

111

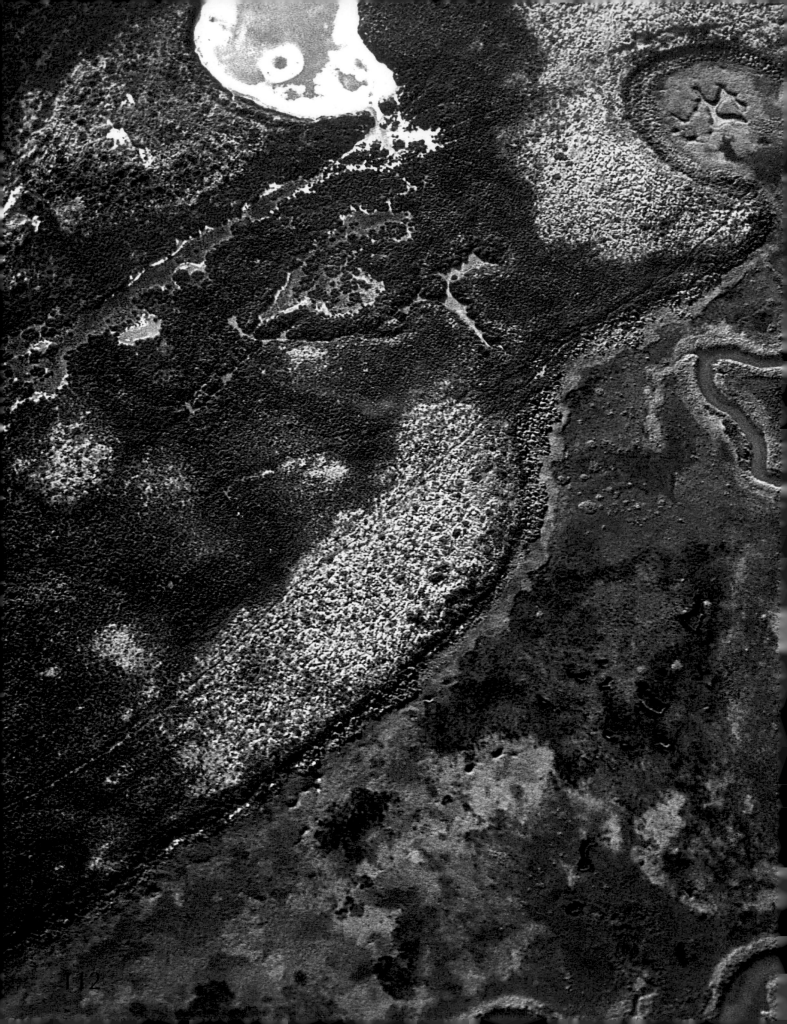

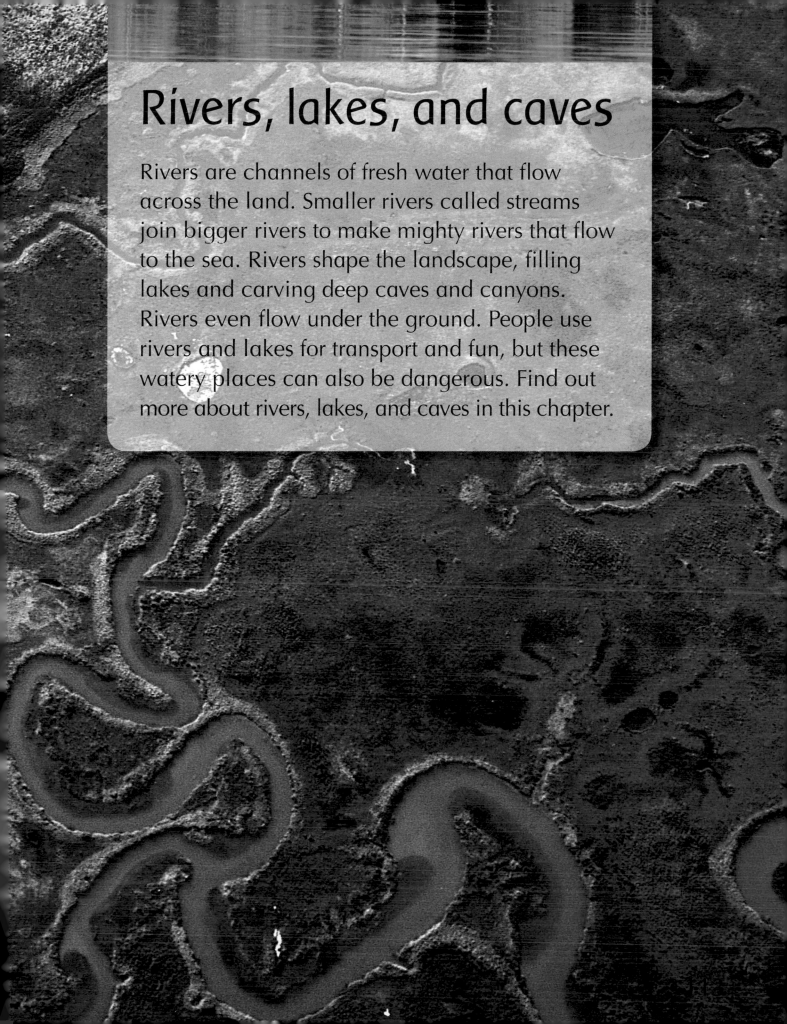

Rivers, lakes, and caves

Rivers are channels of fresh water that flow across the land. Smaller rivers called streams join bigger rivers to make mighty rivers that flow to the sea. Rivers shape the landscape, filling lakes and carving deep caves and canyons. Rivers even flow under the ground. People use rivers and lakes for transport and fun, but these watery places can also be dangerous. Find out more about rivers, lakes, and caves in this chapter.

A river's journey

A river's course is the long journey that it takes from where it begins, high in hills or mountains, to where it ends—in the sea or a lake.

The source

The place where a river starts is called the source. The water comes from rain or melted snow. It may bubble up out of the ground at a spring or trickle out of a lake or glacier.

A stream flows down a mountain.

Course of a river

In its upper course, a river rushes down from a hill or mountain, carving deep gorges and valleys. In its middle and lower courses, a river makes wider valleys and creates flat areas called floodplains.

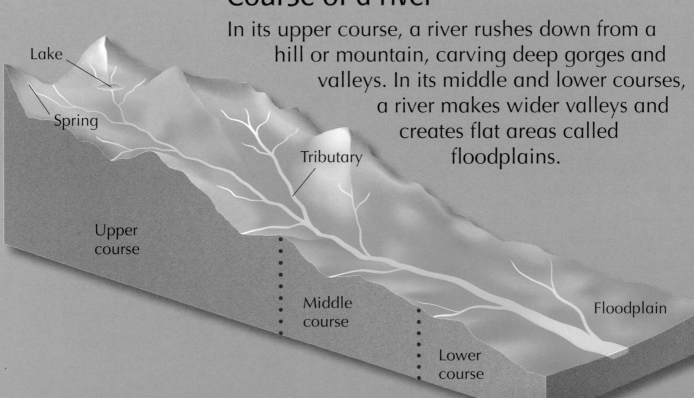

Lake

Spring

Tributary

Upper course

Middle course

Lower course

Floodplain

114

Wearing and shaping

As rivers flow downhill, they carry loose stones and rocks along with them. The stones bounce along the bottom of the river and scrape more soil and rocks away.

A bear walks across the rocks and stones left by a mountain river.

DID YOU KNOW?

The Nile River is the world's longest river. It begins in the mountains of East Africa and flows north for 4,160 miles (6,695 km). The Nile empties into the Mediterranean Sea.

Joining the river

Trickles of water join to make streams. Streams join to make rivers. Lower down, small rivers called tributaries join the main river. The water gets wider and deeper.

Young rivers

At its upper course, a river is known as a young river as it flows downhill. The rushing water loosens rocks and soil, carving deep canyons and gorges.

The Grand Canyon

Canyons form where water cuts through hard rock. The Grand Canyon is a famous canyon in Arizona. The Colorado River has worn a very deep valley as it has cut down through the rock.

Deepest gorge

A gorge is a steep-sided canyon. The Kali Gandaki Gorge in the Himalayas is 3½ miles (5.5 km) deep, the deepest gorge in the world. The river has cut a deep valley between two mountains.

The deep valley of the Grand Canyon.

Leaping salmon

Salmon swim up young mountain rivers to lay their eggs. They have to swim very hard against the flow of water. When they reach fast-moving water, they leap out of the water to move upstream.

These salmon are leaping up a waterfall.

Foaming rapids

Rapids form where young rivers plunge over stones and boulders. The white, foaming water rushes along very quickly. It is fun to ride the rapids in a rubber boat.

Waterfalls

Where a river plunges over a steep cliff, it forms a waterfall. Beautiful falls with white, foaming water can be seen on rivers in many parts of the world.

This boat takes tourists to see the waterfall up close.

Niagara Falls

Niagara Falls is a famous waterfall in North America. It lies on the border between the United States and Canada. The falls curve around like a giant horseshoe and are 180 feet (55 m) high.

How waterfalls form

Waterfalls form where water flows from hard rock onto softer rock. The softer rock wears away more quickly to make a shelf. Water gushing over the shelf carves a pool at the bottom.

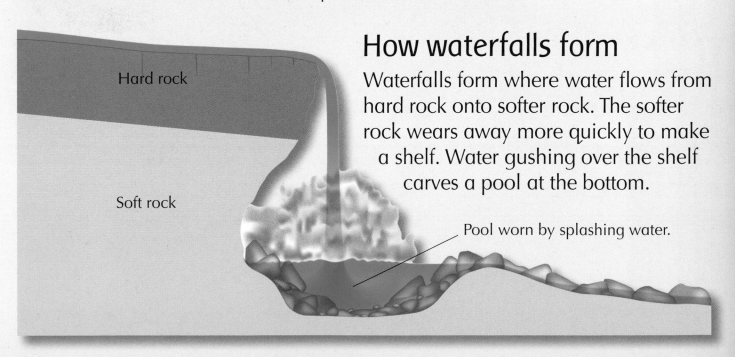

Hard rock

Soft rock

Pool worn by splashing water.

Angel Falls

Angel Falls in Venezuela, South America, is the world's highest waterfall. It is 3,182 feet (970 m) tall and is located were the Churún River plunges over a steep cliff.

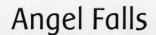

DID YOU KNOW?

Angel Falls is named after American pilot Jimmy Angel, who saw the waterfall from his plane in 1933.

Iguacú swifts

Iguacú Falls is a very beautiful waterfall in South America. It is 2½ miles (4 km) wide and drops nearly 330 feet (100 m). Small birds called swifts nest on the rockface behind the falls. The birds fly through the water to get to their nests.

In the valley

In the middle and lower parts of its journey, the river leaves the hills behind and flows through a wide, flattish valley.

Fertile soil

A river carries mud and gravel. After heavy rain, the river may flood and spill muddy water on to the surrounding land, the floodplain. Crops grow well in the fertile soil of the floodplain.

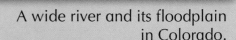

A wide river and its floodplain in Colorado.

River life

Different plants and animals live in and by the river at each stage in its journey. Herons, such as this one, hunt fish and frogs along the banks of gently flowing rivers.

120

River loops are called meanders.

Twisting and turning

Rivers twist and turn as they flow through wide valleys. Water flows fastest on the outside of bends, cutting the bank away. Mud is dropped on the inside, where the flow is weaker. In time, gentle curves become deep loops.

Fastest river flow.

1

Loop

River cuts into the outside of bends.

River cuts through the loop.

2

Oxbow lake forms.

Oxbow lakes

Over many years, the loops get bigger and bigger. Eventually, the river cuts right through the loop. The cut-off part becomes a small lake called an oxbow lake.

121

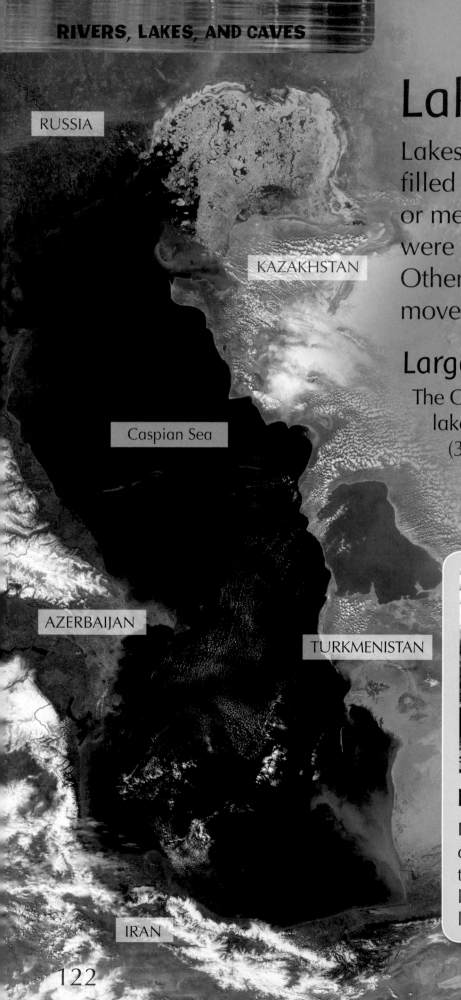

RUSSIA

KAZAKHSTAN

Caspian Sea

AZERBAIJAN

TURKMENISTAN

IRAN

Lakes

Lakes are hollows in the ground filled with water from rivers or melted ice. Some hollows were carved by glaciers. Others formed because of movements in Earth's crust.

Largest lake

The Caspian Sea is the world's largest lake. It covers 143,250 square miles (371,000 sq km) in western Asia. Because the lake contains salty water, it is really an inland sea.

Deepest lake

Lake Baikal in Russia is the world's deepest lake. In places, it is more than 5,575 feet (1,700 m) deep. This lake is home to the only seal that lives in fresh water—the Baikal seal.

122

Highest lake

Lake Titicaca in Peru is the highest lake in the world on which boats sail. It lies 10,170 feet (3,100 m) up in the Andes Mountains. Local people travel in boats such as this one, made of reeds.

Crater lakes

Some lakes form when water fills the crater of a volcano. Crater Lake (below) in Oregon is 1,942 feet (592 m) deep. It is the deepest lake in the United States.

Pink flamingoes feeding in an estuary.

Reaching the sea

The place where a river meets the sea is called its mouth. The river's flow slows as it reaches the sea, and it drops its load of sand or mud to form flat areas called estuaries or deltas.

River estuary

The estuary is the lower part of a river, where fresh water mixes with salty seawater. Worms and snails burrow in the muddy banks, providing plenty of food for birds.

Deltas

A delta forms when mud or sand builds up at a river's mouth. The delta may be triangular or shaped like a bird's foot. The river divides into many smaller channels as it flows through the delta.

The delta of the Mississippi River is shaped like a bird's foot.

124

Nile Delta

The Nile River has a huge, fan-shaped delta. Mud dumped by the river has made a triangle of fertile land. Green fields are surrounded by desert, which looks brown.

Mediterranean Sea

Nile Delta

Red Sea

EGYPT

Nile River

DID YOU KNOW?

The world's largest delta is the Ganges Delta in Asia. It covers 46,600 square miles (75,000 sq km) and has about 250 miles (400 km) of coastline.

Nile crocodile

In the past, the Nile Delta was home to the Nile crocodile. Now farms cover the delta, and these fierce beasts are rarely seen there. They are still found in rivers, estuaries, and deltas in other parts of Africa.

The mighty Amazon

The Amazon River in South America is not as long as the Nile, but it contains far more water. The river begins high in the Andes Mountains and flows through the Amazon rain forest on its way to the sea.

Amazon facts

- The Amazon flows for about 4,000 miles (6,450 km). The river and its tributaries cover more than 2.7 million square miles (7 million sq km) – more than a third of South America.

- Every second, the Amazon empties 196,200 cubic yards (150,000 cu m) of water into the ocean. That's enough to fill 75 Olympic-sized pools.

River basin

Water from an area 10 times the size of France flows into the Amazon. The total area through which a river and its tributaries flow is called the river's basin.

Amazon Delta

The Amazon measures about 200 miles (300 km) across as it reaches the ocean. The river is so wide that it looks like the sea. This picture shows water weaving between islands in the Amazon Delta.

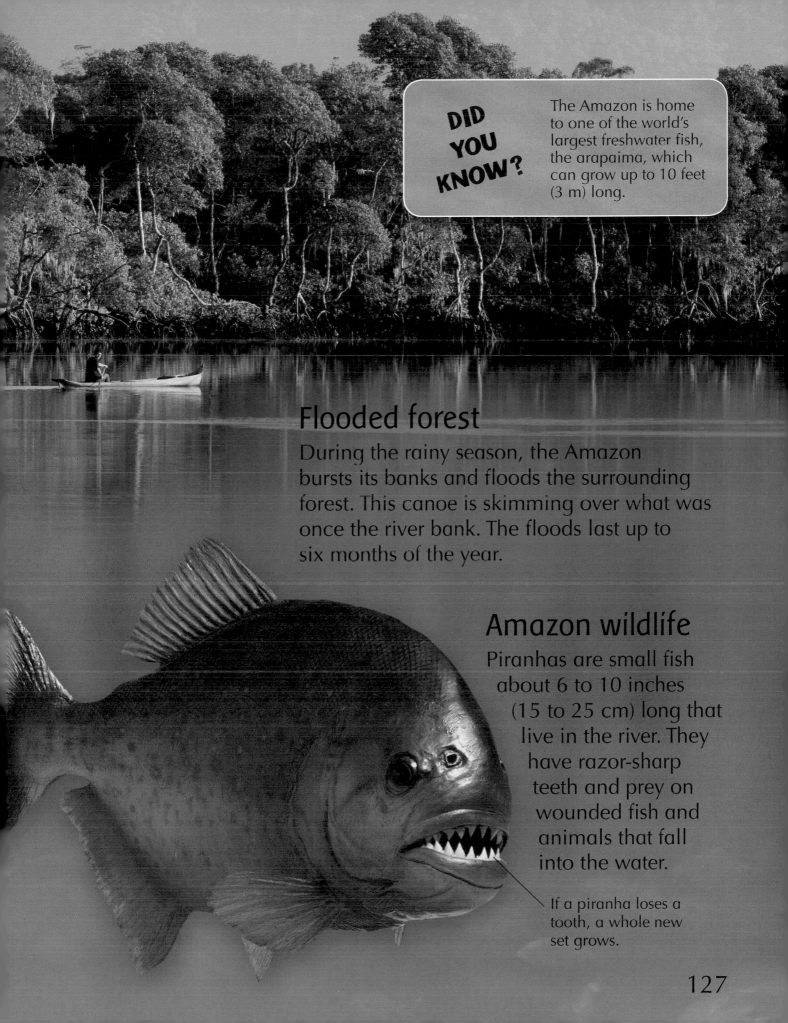

Flooded forest

During the rainy season, the Amazon bursts its banks and floods the surrounding forest. This canoe is skimming over what was once the river bank. The floods last up to six months of the year.

Amazon wildlife

Piranhas are small fish about 6 to 10 inches (15 to 25 cm) long that live in the river. They have razor-sharp teeth and prey on wounded fish and animals that fall into the water.

If a piranha loses a tooth, a whole new set grows.

127

Underground rivers

Water flows under the ground as well as over it. Water running under the ground can wear away some types of rock to make deep, dark caves.

Gaping Gill, a sinkhole in England, is 364 feet (111 m) deep.

Disappearing water

Water eats into a type of soft rock called limestone. Over time, it makes deep holes called sinkholes and runs under the ground. The water wears away the rock beneath the surface, forming hollow caves.

Limestone caves

Water can form huge caves in limestone rock, linked by underground tunnels. Water falling through sinkholes can carve out deep pools. Rock formations called stalactites and stalagmites (see page 130) are often seen in caves.

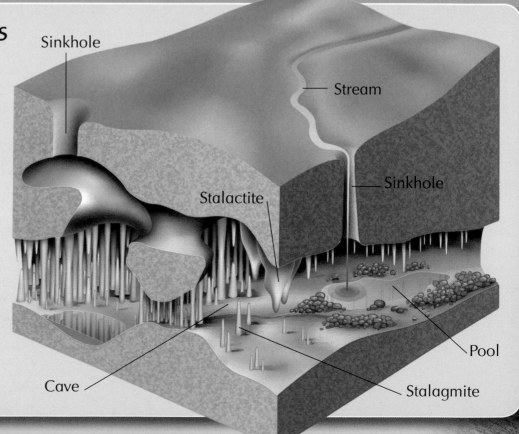

Sinkhole

Stream

Stalactite

Sinkhole

Cave

Pool

Stalagmite

128

Wells

If you dig down deep enough anywhere on Earth, you will reach water. People dig holes called wells and lower buckets down them to bring water to the surface.

Desert oasis

Water cannot soak through all types of rock. When it reaches a layer of rock it cannot pass through, water runs sideways. Sometimes the water reaches the surface again and bubbles out in a spring. In a desert, this place is called an oasis.

A boy draws water from a well in Afghanistan, Asia.

An oasis in Libya, Africa.

Stalagmites rise from the floor.

Stalactites hang down from the ceiling.

Amazing caves

In some places on Earth, a secret world lies underground, where caves and tunnels run for miles. Exploring this hidden world is called spelunking.

Stalagmites and stalactites

Stalagmites and stalactites are stony pillars found in caves. They are made by dripping water. The water contains a mineral called calcite, which builds up to make the pillars.

Spelunkers

Spelunkers wear waterproof clothes and a helmet with a light on when they explore these dark, wet places. This spelunker is looking at a stalactite.

130

Bat caves

Many bats like dark places. They sleep in caves by day and hunt for food at night. Bats hang upside down from cave walls, using their sharp claws.

Cave paintings

In prehistoric times, some people lived in caves. They painted pictures of the animals they hunted on cave walls. This painting in a French cave is more than 15,000 years old.

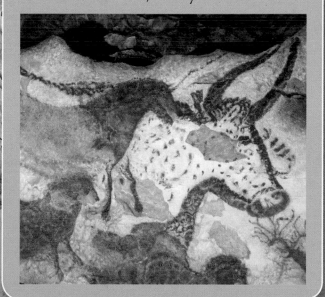

DID YOU KNOW?

The largest group of linked caves and tunnels is the Mammoth Cave System in Kentucky. The caves run for 348 miles (560 km).

Using rivers

Rivers provide water for drinking, washing, and cleaning. People also use rivers to water crops, run factories, and make electricity. No wonder people live near rivers all over the world.

Water for farming

River water is vital for farming. These green fields by the Nile River are watered by the river. Without the Nile, this place would be a desert.

Cities on rivers

Most of the world's oldest towns and villages were built by rivers. Some of these are now capital cities, such as London and Paris. The Houses of Parliament (below) in London are next to the Thames River.

Water for energy

Hydroelectric stations use energy from fast-flowing water to make electricity. A dam is often built to control the flow of water. This is Glen Canyon Dam in Arizona.

Factories by rivers

Factories of all kinds use river water to power machinery, and also for cleaning. Paper mills, like this one, use huge amounts of water every day.

DID YOU KNOW?

Glen Canyon Dam is 708 feet (216 m) high. A huge lake called Lake Powell has built up behind the dam. The lake supplies water to nearby cities.

133

Travel and fun

Rivers have been used by people to travel or move goods ever since boats were invented. Rivers and lakes are also great places to have fun.

River transport

Paddleboats, such as this one, have sailed the Mississippi River since the early 1800s. They carry passengers and cargo. This boat is taking tourists on a sight-seeing trip.

Canals

Canals are human-made waterways. People dig canals to link rivers, lakes, or seas. In Central America, the Panama Canal cuts across a narrow strip of land to link the Pacific and Atlantic oceans.

Huge cargo ships on the Panama Canal.

Crossing rivers

In some places, bridges have to be built to carry road and railroad traffic over rivers. This bridge in Bristol, England, crosses the River Avon. Motorists have to pay a fee to use the bridge.

Water sports

Rivers and lakes are used for many sports, such as canoeing, sailing, fishing, and windsurfing. This boy is paddling a type of canoe called a kayak.

DID YOU KNOW?

The world's longest bridge is the Akashi Kaiko Bridge in Japan. It links two islands and is nearly 2½ miles (4 km) long.

River safety

Rivers can be dangerous places. Floods can strike after heavy rain, damaging roads and houses. Dirty river water can also harm people and animals.

These people are stacking sandbags to try to keep the Mississippi floodwater away from their homes.

Mississippi floods

In 1993, the Mississippi River burst its banks. Floodwater covered more than 17,000 square miles (44,000 sq km). About 70,000 people had to leave their homes.

Floods in China

When the Yangtze River in China flooded in 1998, this family escaped by boat. Unfortunately, more than 3,000 people died and about 14 million were made homeless.

Water pollution

River water can be polluted (made dirty) by sewage or waste from farms and factories. This can harm people. Many countries now have strict rules to stop river pollution.

This pipe is emptying dirty water into a river.

Preventing floods

During very high tides (see pages 142–143), seawater could flood London. The Thames Barrier was built to protect the city. It has huge gates that can be shut to prevent seawater flowing into the river.

Seas and oceans

The oceans are a vast world that we are still exploring and finding out about. This chapter will explain how waves, tides, and currents affect the ocean and shape the land. It will tell you how coasts, islands, and coral reefs form. You can also find out about the creatures that live at different depths in the oceans, including the deep sea—a mysterious world that we know very little about.

Watery world

Only one third of Earth's surface is land. Salty water covers the rest. This huge expanse of water is divided into areas called oceans and seas.

Salty oceans

Ocean water is salty because it contains minerals carried out to sea by rivers. The main minerals are sodium and chloride. These two minerals make salt.

DID YOU KNOW? The Pacific Ocean is the world's biggest ocean. It covers 64 million sq miles (166 million sq km) and holds over half of all the water in the oceans.

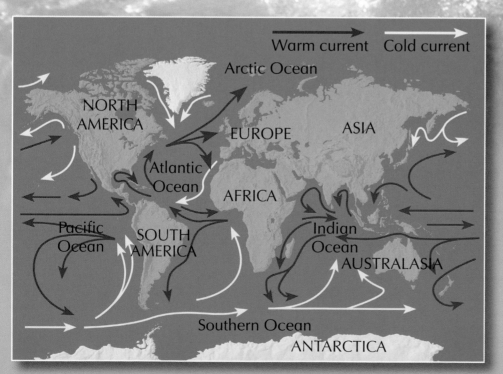

Warm current   Cold current

Arctic Ocean

NORTH AMERICA

EUROPE   ASIA

Atlantic Ocean

AFRICA

Pacific Ocean

SOUTH AMERICA

Indian Ocean

AUSTRALASIA

Southern Ocean

ANTARCTICA

Oceans and seas

The five oceans are called the Atlantic, Pacific, Indian, Arctic, and Southern oceans. They are linked by smaller areas of water called seas. Warm and cold currents flow like mighty rivers through the oceans.

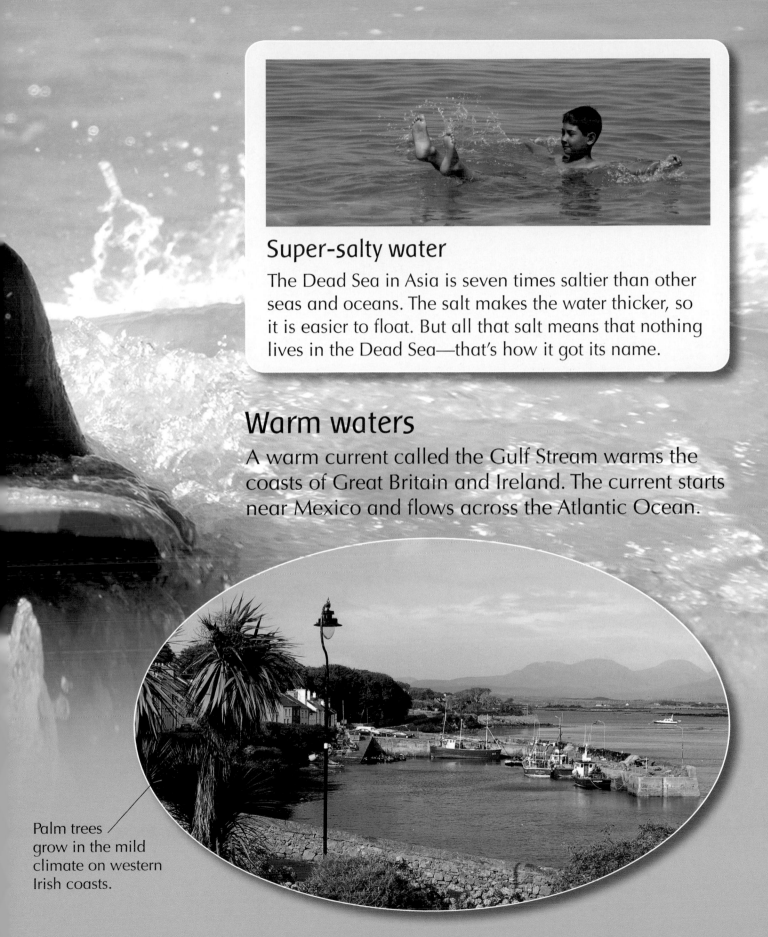

Super-salty water

The Dead Sea in Asia is seven times saltier than other seas and oceans. The salt makes the water thicker, so it is easier to float. But all that salt means that nothing lives in the Dead Sea—that's how it got its name.

Warm waters

A warm current called the Gulf Stream warms the coasts of Great Britain and Ireland. The current starts near Mexico and flows across the Atlantic Ocean.

Palm trees grow in the mild climate on western Irish coasts.

Waves and tides

The water in seas and oceans is always on the move. Waves sweep across the ocean surface. The sea rises and falls on coasts as tides come and go.

How do waves form?

Winds blowing across the ocean make ripples on the surface. The ripples grow into waves. Far from land, low waves roll across the ocean. Waves get taller as they reach the coast.

Circling water

The water in a wave moves in a circle. Far out to sea, the water circles freely. Close to shore, the seabed stops water from flowing in circles. This makes the waves rise up into crests.

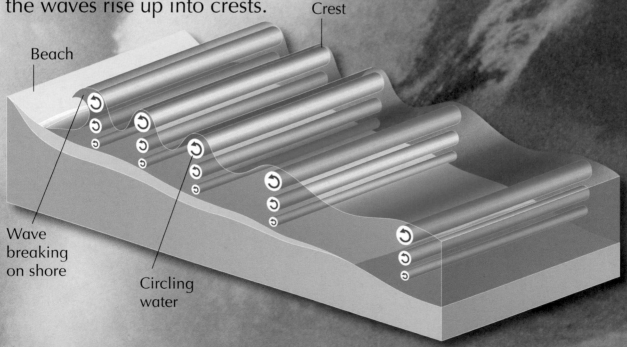

Crest

Beach

Wave breaking on shore

Circling water

142

Changing tides

Tides mainly happen because the Moon's gravity (see pages 16–17) pulls on the oceans. As the Moon circles Earth, it pulls the sea toward it. A mound of water forms below the Moon—this mound is high tide.

A surfer rides a huge wave.

High and low tides

These pictures show the same harbor in Cornwall, England, at high and low tides. At high tide, water fills the harbor. At low tide, the harbor is empty, and the boats are stranded on the sand.

High tide

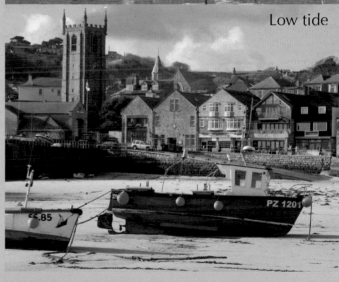

Low tide

DID YOU KNOW?

The Bay of Fundy in Canada has very high and very low tides. The water level changes by up to 52½ feet (16 m).

Rocky coasts

High cliffs tower above the sea on some coastlines. Other shores have wide, sandy bays, headlands, or amazing rock arches. All of these landscapes are formed by the pounding waves.

Steep cliffs

Waves crash onto the shore every minute of every day. Water, grit, and pebbles smash against rocky coasts, chipping pieces away. Steep cliffs form where hills meet the ocean.

Headlands and bays

As waves beat against the shore, soft rocks wear away more quickly than hard rocks. The sea cuts deep, curving bays into soft rocks. Hard rocks stand up to the waves, forming headlands that stick far out to sea.

Headland

Bay

Rock arch

Rock arches form where waves eat into a headland from both sides. This makes two caves, which eventually wear all the way through to make an arch. This arch is in the Galapagos Islands in South America.

Arch is worn by the waves.

Direction of waves

Arch collapses to leave a stack.

DID YOU KNOW?
Waves pound into cliffs and slowly wear them away. On some coasts, the land is worn away by more than 3 feet (1m) each year.

How stacks form

Waves continue to crash against a rock arch. Eventually, the top of the arch crumbles, leaving a pillar of rock standing in the ocean. The pillar is called a stack.

On the beach

Beaches can be sandy or pebbly. Most people prefer a sandy beach to any other kind of beach— and some animals do, too!

How do beaches form?

Rivers carry sand and rocks out to sea. Waves also chip pieces off cliffs. Beaches form where waves dump the sand and rocks in sheltered bays.

Sandy or pebbly

Sand is made of tiny parts of rock or shell. Rivers and waves have smashed the rocks and shells into tiny pieces. Pebbles on beaches are small rocks that have been worn smooth by the water.

A sandy beach has formed in this bay in Cornwall, England.

Beach wildlife

All types of animals live on beaches. Crabs, worms, and cockles burrow into the sand. Gulls search for fish by the water's edge. Shellfish, such as limpets, cling to the rocks.

Crabs have large claws, which they use to grab food.

Shifting sideways

Where waves strike the shore at an angle, they shift sand and pebbles sideways. This material can pile up out at sea to make a strip of land called a spit. Groins are fences built across a beach to stop the sand from moving along the beach.

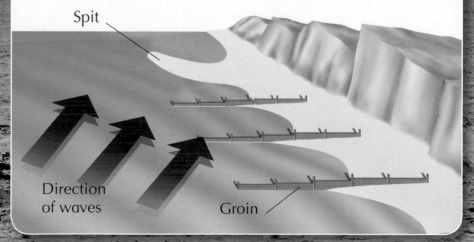

Spit

Direction of waves

Groin

Islands

Islands are areas of land totally surrounded by water. Some islands, such as Great Britain, are big, but many islands are small. There are islands in rivers and lakes, as well as in the sea.

Volcanic islands

Islands that lie far out to sea are often the tips of underwater volcanoes. The volcano erupts on the seabed and lava builds up to make a mountain. The mountain eventually breaks the water's surface, forming an island.

Near the mainland

Some islands lie close to large land masses called continents. Great Britain was once joined to mainland Europe but became an island when the sea level rose thousands of years ago.

Ireland

Great Britain

Europe

A volcanic island in Alaska.

A ring of coral

Coral islands

This island is made of a hard material called coral (see pages 150–151). Sometimes a ring of coral forms around a small volcanic island. The island may later sink due to movement of Earth's crust, leaving just the coral.

Island life

Many remote islands are home to animals found nowhere else. The giant tortoise lives on a group of islands called the Galapagos Islands in South America.

Great Barrier Reef

Coral reefs form in warm, shallow seas. They aren't made of rock, but are built from small creatures called coral polyps. The Great Barrier Reef off Australia is the world's largest coral reef.

Coral homes

Coral reefs are hard ridges just below the surface of the sea. They are home to many ocean creatures, including colorful fish, shrimp, and starfish. Turtles and sharks swim nearby.

Barrier Reef facts

🌐 The Great Barrier Reef is made up of 2,500 smaller reefs. The reef stretches for about 1,250 miles (2,000 km), and it is so large that it can be seen from space.

🌐 More than 1,500 different types of fish live on the Great Barrier Reef.

Reef builders

A coral polyp has a chalky body and armlike tentacles. When a polyp dies, its chalky body remains. Millions of bodies build up on top of one another to form a coral reef.

Coral tentacles

Reef stingers

Sea anemones live on the reef. The stings of these animals kill most fish, but clownfish are safe because their bodies are protected by a special slime.

DID YOU KNOW?

Coral only grows a few inches a year. It takes millions of years for a large reef to form.

Scary sharks

Sharks hunt in the clear waters by the reef. These big fish have a very good sense of smell. When they smell the blood of a wounded creature, they swim up for the kill.

Pointed fin sticks out of the water when a shark swims near the surface.

Jellyfish

Sunlit zone:
0–650 ft.
(0–200 m)

Mackerel

Mid-depths:
650–6,550 ft.
(200–2,000 m)

Sperm
whale

Giant squid

Deep sea:
6,550–
13,100 ft.
(2,000–
4,000 m)

Gulper eel

Anglerfish

Depths below
13,100 ft.
(4,000 m)
are called
the abyss.

Open ocean

In the open ocean, water stretches out on all sides and for several miles downward. The water can be divided into layers, with different creatures living at different depths.

Ocean layers

The upper waters are lit by the Sun. Jellyfish and mackerel swim there. Sperm whales and giant squid swim in the dim mid-waters. Gulper eels and anglerfish live in the inky black depths.

Plankton

Tiny plants and animals called plankton float on the ocean surface. These creatures are so small you can only see them using a microscope. Plankton provide food for many larger creatures, including whales.

At the surface

Large, powerful fish called marlin chase after the shoals of mackerel on the surface. They snap up the small fish with their long, pointed snouts.

Diving to the depths

Sperm whales come to the surface to breathe. Then they dive to depths of 3,300 feet (1,000 m) to hunt giant squid. Many sperm whales are scarred by battles with squid.

Marlin can swim at speeds of up to 50 miles (80 km) an hour.

DID YOU KNOW?

The ocean's deepest point is the Marianas Trench in the Pacific. It lies 35,827 feet (10,920 m) below the surface. In 1961, two scientists went to the bottom in a submarine.

153

On the seabed

Many creatures live on the seabed. Starfish and flatfish live in fairly shallow water. Other creatures lurk on the bed of the deep oceans, where there are mountains, cliffs, and volcanoes similar to those on land.

Flatfish

Flatfish rest on the seabed. The speckled colors of this plaice blend in with the sand. The fish changes color when it moves on to rock or weeds, allowing it to hide from its enemies.

Ocean floor

Long mountain chains run down the center of the oceans. The flat plains on either side may be dotted with volcanoes or cut by deep trenches. The seabed slopes upward to broad, flat shelves that edge the land.

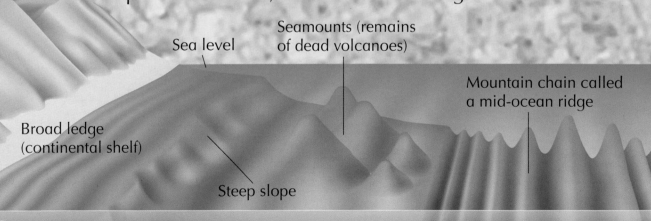

Sea level

Seamounts (remains of dead volcanoes)

Mountain chain called a mid-ocean ridge

Broad ledge (continental shelf)

Steep slope

Plain

154

Starfish

Starfish creep along the seabed. Most starfish have five arms, but some have up to 20. A starfish can regrow an arm if it is bitten off by an enemy.

Mapping the seabed

Scientists map the seabed using a technique called sonar. They aim sound waves at the bottom and listen to the echoes that bounce back. The time taken by the echoes tells them how deep it is.

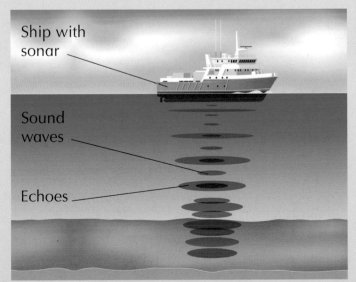

Ship with sonar

Sound waves

Echoes

Plain

Deep trench

The deep sea

The deep sea is the last unexplored place on Earth because it is so difficult to get to. Only a few submarines can descend that deep.

Deep-sea submarine

This special submarine can explore the bottom of the ocean. It is called *Alvin* and carries three people. *Alvin* has two arms that can collect samples.

Black smokers

In 1977, scientists exploring a deep-sea ridge made an amazing discovery. They found strange chimneys spouting clouds of black, boiling-hot water. These undersea volcanoes are called black smokers.

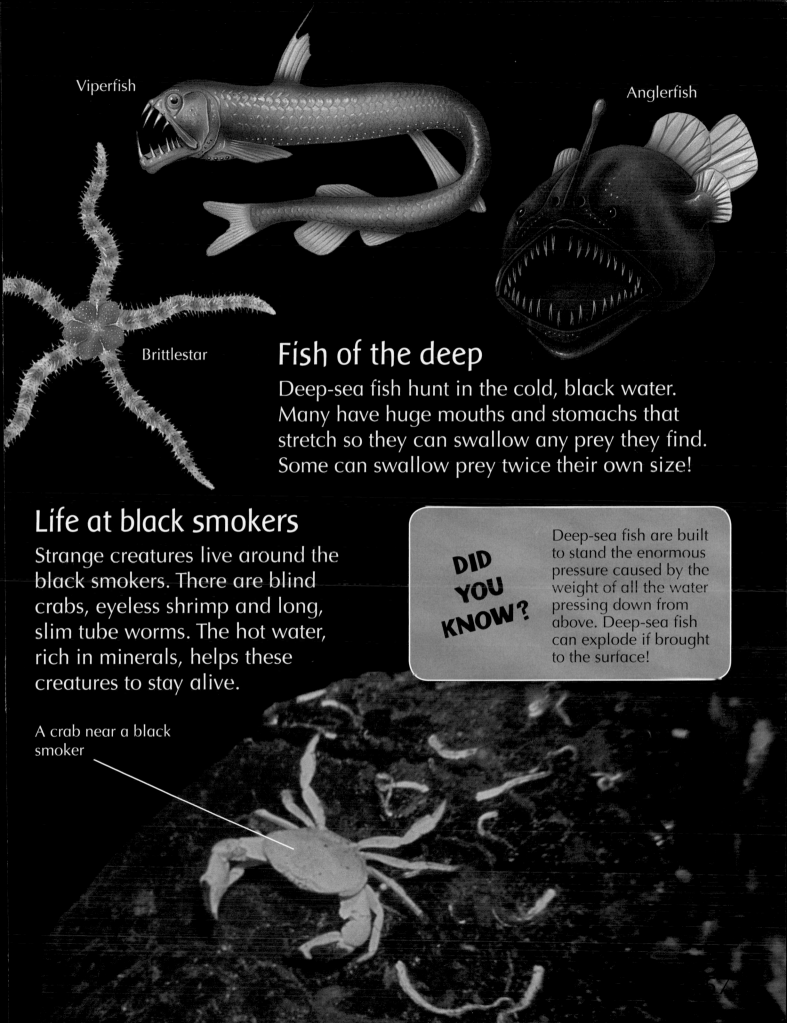

Viperfish

Anglerfish

Brittlestar

Fish of the deep

Deep-sea fish hunt in the cold, black water.
Many have huge mouths and stomachs that
stretch so they can swallow any prey they find.
Some can swallow prey twice their own size!

Life at black smokers

Strange creatures live around the
black smokers. There are blind
crabs, eyeless shrimp and long,
slim tube worms. The hot water,
rich in minerals, helps these
creatures to stay alive.

A crab near a black
smoker

DID YOU KNOW?

Deep-sea fish are built
to stand the enormous
pressure caused by the
weight of all the water
pressing down from
above. Deep-sea fish
can explode if brought
to the surface!

Icy seas

The seas in the polar regions are covered with ice for much of the year. There are towering icebergs and huge, flat-topped ice shelves. When the sea freezes over, a different type of ice—pack ice—forms.

Ice shelf

Huge ice shelves edge the land in the polar regions. They form where glaciers meet the ocean, and the ice breaks off and floats out to sea.

A thick coat of feathers keeps out the cold.

Penguins

Penguins live on the coasts of Antarctica. They walk with a waddle on land, but are fast swimmers. They dive into the icy water to hunt fish. Penguins cannot fly, but they flap their wings to swim underwater.

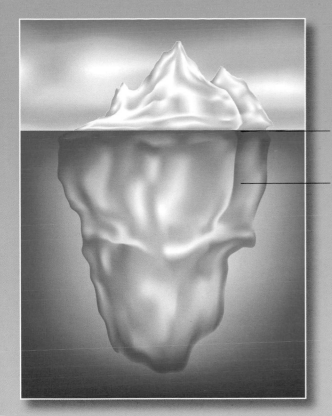

Sea level

Four-fifths of an iceberg lies below the surface.

Icebergs

Icebergs form when a large chunk of ice breaks off an ice shelf or a glacier. Icebergs can be a danger to ships. Only a small part of an iceberg shows above the surface—the rest is below.

DID YOU KNOW?

The biggest iceberg ever seen had a surface area the size of Belgium! Icebergs can be up to 500 feet (150 m) high.

Sinking of the *Titanic*

In 1912, a luxury passenger ship called the *Titanic* hit an iceberg in the North Atlantic Ocean. The ship sank in just four hours, and 1,500 people drowned. The *Titanic*'s owners had claimed it was unsinkable!

Ocean treasures

All types of riches come from the ocean. As well as fish and shellfish, there are valuable minerals, such as oil and gas. Harvesting the ocean's riches, however, is often easier said than done!

Fishing boats

Fishermen set traps and nets to catch fish and shellfish. Different nets are used to catch fish at the surface and on the bottom. Modern fishing boats catch so many fish that some fish are now rare.

Pearls

Pearls are valuable gems made by shellfish called oysters. When a piece of grit gets inside an oyster's shell, a hard, shiny ball, called a pearl, forms around the grit. Diving deep for pearls can be dangerous.

A pearl diver collects oysters from baskets in Thailand.

Oil and gas

Oil and gas are mined from the seabed in shallow waters. A platform called a rig may stand on stilts or float, anchored to the bottom. Engineers drill into the seabed to reach the oil or gas, and then pump it to the surface.

Salt

People get salt from the oceans by flooding shallow ponds near the sea with seawater. The water dries in the Sun, leaving behind the salt.

This salt has been raked into piles.

NORTH CORMORANT

DID YOU KNOW?

Many modern fishing boats have refrigerators on board. The fish are frozen soon after being caught to keep them fresh. This allows boats to stay out longer at sea.

161

The kraken

Legends tell of a sea monster called the kraken. The tales said it would trap ships in its tentacles and drag them down to the seabed. Experts believe these stories were based on the giant squid.

Mysteries of the ocean

The undersea world holds many mysteries and also dangers. In past times, stories of sea monsters helped to explain the dangers. We now understand a lot more about the oceans, but some mysteries remain.

Rocky reefs

Rocks and sandbanks can be very dangerous for ships, especially in fog or storms. Lighthouses warn ships away from the rocks. In the past, lighthouse keepers controlled the lights, but now most lighthouses work automatically.

In 1872, a ship called the *Mary Celeste* was found drifting in the Atlantic Ocean. The crew and passengers had all vanished. No one has fully explained this mystery.

Myth of the mermaid

In days gone by, sailors reported seeing mermaids. These legendary creatures were said to look like women with a fish's tail. Experts believe the stories are based on sightings of real, seal-like creatures called dugongs.

This statue of a mermaid is in Copenhagen harbor, Denmark.

Diving for treasure

In dangerous waters, wrecks of sunken ships lie on the seabed. Some ships sank carrying gold, silver, and jewels. Divers search the wrecks and sometimes bring treasure to the surface.

163

Air and weather

Weather is created by the Sun heating the Earth, which makes the air move around. This produces constantly changing conditions, from clear blue skies to gusting winds and deafening thunderstorms. This chapter will explain about air and weather. Find out how clouds form and why it rains. Discover how animals and people cope with different weather. Learn how experts can predict the weather.

The atmosphere

Earth is wrapped in a protective blanket of gases called the atmosphere. This blanket makes life possible on Earth. Our weather is created in the lowest layer.

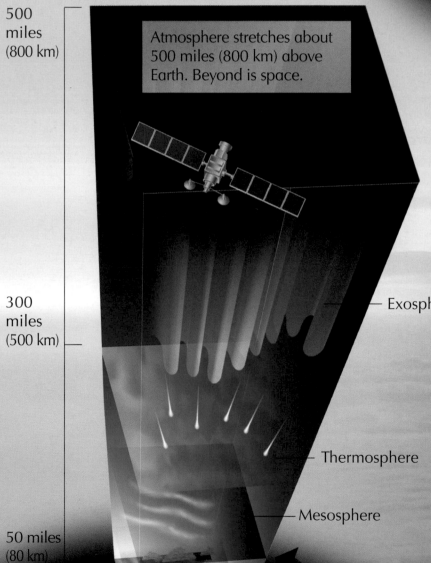

500 miles (800 km)

Atmosphere stretches about 500 miles (800 km) above Earth. Beyond is space.

300 miles (500 km)

— Exosphere

— Thermosphere

— Mesosphere

50 miles (80 km)

0 miles (0 km)

Stratosphere

Troposphere

Blanket of gases

The main atmosphere gases are nitrogen and also oxygen, which is vital for life. Small amounts of other gases help to trap the Sun's heat and filter out harmful rays. Earth's gravity keeps the atmosphere in place.

Layers of atmosphere

The atmosphere has five layers stacked on top of one another. The lowest, the troposphere, contains about 75 percent of the atmosphere's gases. The air thins out as you head toward the exosphere and space.

Thin air

The higher you go, the less oxygen there is. Mountaineers use bottled oxygen in the "thin air" to help them breathe. The air on the highest mountains contains about one third of the gases found at sea level.

Above the clouds

Clouds form in the lowest layer of the atmosphere. Planes can climb to the next layer, the stratosphere, to get above the clouds and avoid storms.

Top of cloud cover

DID YOU KNOW?

Earth's atmosphere helps protect us from meteors—rocks falling from space. Meteors usually burn up high in the atmosphere, forming "shooting stars."

1% other gases

21% oxygen

78% nitrogen

Air

The air in the atmosphere contains a mixture of gases. The constant recycling of these gases links the atmosphere to the living world of plants, animals, and humans.

What is air made of?

This balloon shows the amounts of gases that make up air. There is almost four times as much nitrogen as oxygen. The other gases include carbon dioxide and water vapor.

Plant life

Trees and plants use carbon dioxide, water, and sunlight to grow in a process called photosynthesis. They give off oxygen as waste. Nitrogen in the soil helps to nourish plants.

DID YOU KNOW?

The balance of gases in the atmosphere has remained the same for about a billion years.

Animal life

Living creatures need oxygen to live. When we breathe in, oxygen passes from our lungs into our blood. Blood is pumped all around our body and provides the oxygen we need to live, move, and grow. We breathe out carbon dioxide as waste.

Horses breathe in oxygen and breathe out carbon dioxide, just as we do.

Breathing underwater

Fish also need oxygen to live. They take oxygen from water, using feathery structures called gills. As water passes over the gills, they filter off the oxygen.

This slit leads to the fish's gills.

Light as air

Air is light. However, the weight of all the air above presses down on you. This is known as air pressure. You can't feel the air pushing against you because the air inside you pushes back. But you can see its effects.

Floating and falling

If you drop a ball and a feather, the ball reaches the ground first. Both are pulled by gravity, but the air pushes against the wispy feather more than the smooth, curved ball, so the ball falls faster.

Blowing bubbles

When you blow soapy bubbles, warm air from your lungs fills the bubbles. Warm air is lighter than cold air, so the bubbles drift upward. They sink as the air inside cools.

Hot-air balloon

A hot-air balloon climbs high in the sky because a burner heats the air inside the balloon. This makes the balloon lighter than the surrounding air, so the balloon rises.

Rising air

When the Sun heats a mass of air, the warm air starts to rise. This creates a current of warm, rising air called a thermal. Birds use thermals to glide for hours, hardly flapping their wings.

Gull's large wings help it glide on thermals.

Basket below the balloon carries people.

DID YOU KNOW? Hang gliders are like large kites that pilots hang from to fly through the air. They use thermals to rise high in the sky.

171

Wind

Wind is moving air. The wind blows when the Sun heats Earth's surface unevenly. Moving air brings different kinds of weather, such as clouds and rain.

Why do winds blow?

Warm air weighs less than cold air and rises. Cooler air rushes in to fill the space left by the warm air. This movement of air is what makes the wind blow.

You need a strong wind to fly a kite!

Wind speed

A wind's strength depends on its speed. A slow wind rustles leaves. A medium wind will make flags flutter. A very fast wind can sometimes uproot trees.

Using the wind

People use the wind in many ways. Wind turns the sails of windmills. The moving sails turn a grindstone, which crushes wheat into flour. Wind also pushes on the sails of yachts, making them move across the sea.

Wooden sail

Weather vanes

Weather vanes, such as this one, turn to show which way the wind is blowing. In most areas, the wind usually blows from one direction. This is called the prevailing wind.

DID YOU KNOW?

Modern windmills called wind turbines use energy from the wind to make electricity. The sails turn generators, which produce electricity.

Cloudy skies

Clouds are masses of floating moisture. They are made of millions of tiny water drops or ice crystals. Clouds form when warm air containing moisture rises and cools.

Cumulus clouds drift across the sky in summer.

Fluffy cumulus

If you watch the sky, you will see clouds of different shapes. Different clouds bring different types of weather. White, fluffy clouds known as cumulus usually mean fine weather.

Flat-topped
cumulonimbus
clouds

Wispy cirrus

Cirrus clouds form very high in the sky. They are made from ice crystals. The wind sometimes blows these white clouds into wispy shapes, such as horses' tails.

Storm clouds

Cumulonimbus clouds are towering, flat-topped clouds. If you see these clouds, watch out for bad weather! They often bring heavy rain, hail, or thunderstorms (see pages 202–203 and 210–211).

Thick, gray stratus
clouds

Thick stratus

Stratus clouds are low-level clouds. Sometimes they cover the whole sky in a thick gray blanket. These clouds may bring drizzle, rain, or snow.

DID YOU KNOW?

Cirrus are the highest clouds. They form 3¾–7½ miles (6–12 km) up in the sky. Cumulonimbus clouds are very tall and can tower up to 5½ miles (9 km) high.

It's raining!

Sooner or later, clouds shed their moisture as rain, snow, sleet, or hail. This is called precipitation. Very fine rain is called drizzle. A short burst of rain is called a shower.

Rain from ice

In very high clouds, the moisture forms ice instead of water. Tiny ice crystals join up to make snowflakes. Snowflakes often melt on the way down to fall as rain.

Rainstorm

Tiny drops of water in clouds join together to make bigger drops. When the raindrops become too heavy they fall to the ground. A very heavy shower is called a cloudburst.

The sky turns gray when the clouds become thick.

Rainbows

If the sun comes out when it's raining, you may see a rainbow. Raindrops bend the different colors in white light, separating them out into red, orange, yellow, green, blue, indigo, and violet.

Keeping dry

A raincoat and rubber boots will keep you dry in wet weather. An umbrella will keep you extra dry! They are all made of waterproof materials that keep out the rain.

The water cycle

Moisture moves between the air, oceans, and land in a never-ending cycle. As the water moves around, it changes from a liquid into a gas and back again.

Powered by the Sun

The Sun powers the water cycle by warming the air. Warm air holds more moisture than cold air. When warm, moist air cools, clouds form and bring rain.

Sun

2. Warm, moist air blows inland.

1. Moisture rises into the air.

5. Rivers drain into the sea.

Rising moisture

As the Sun warms the sea, moisture rises into the air in the form of a gas called water vapor. This process is known as evaporation. Winds blow the warm, moist air toward the land.

3. Clouds form as warm air rises and cools.

4. Rain falls from clouds and runs into rivers.

Clouds form

When warm, moist air rises over hills or mountains, it cools. The water vapor turns into tiny drops of water or ice, which gather to make clouds. The clouds bring rain, snow, or hail.

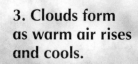

DID YOU KNOW?

The rain that falls where you live has fallen many times before in other places. No new water forms on Earth—it is just recycled naturally.

Soaking up water

When it rains, some water drains into rivers and travels back to the sea. Rainwater also soaks into the ground. Trees draw up moisture through their roots and release it through their leaves.

Dew

Dew forms on thin, cold surfaces in the morning or evening. As the surface cools, moisture from the air collects on it. When it's very cold, the dew becomes frost.

Water appears on leaves as dew drops or frost.

Dew, mist, and fog

Dew, mist, and fog all form when moisture in the air collects into water droplets. This happens when the air cools suddenly, for example when it blows over a cold surface.

Mist

Mist is low cloud that touches Earth's surface. Mountains are often misty because the air is colder there.

Llamas roaming in the misty Andes Mountains in Peru.

Fog

Fog is thick mist, where you can see less than about ½ mile (1 km) ahead. Fog can be dangerous. Drivers have to use bright fog lights and be careful when driving.

Smog

Smog is a dirty haze of smoke and fog that hangs over cities. It forms in air that has been polluted by fumes from cars and factories. People who live in smoggy cities can have trouble breathing.

Deserts and drought

Some parts of the world get more rain than others. Deserts are places where almost no rain falls. Some deserts lie near the center of continents where the air is very dry.

Desert plants

Cactus plants can grow in dry places. They store water in thick stems. Saguaro cactuses, such as this one, can grow up to 56 feet (17 m) tall and live for 200 years.

Sharp spikes keep predators away.

Drinking dew

Reptiles, such as snakes and lizards, are common in deserts. This lizard, called a thorny devil, lives in Australian deserts. The spines on its body channel dew toward its mouth for drinking.

Desert in bloom

When rain finally falls in the desert, seeds sprout and plants bloom quickly. For a few days, the desert becomes a carpet of flowers. But the flowers soon wither as dry weather returns.

Drought

A drought is a long time without rain. Some parts of Africa are regularly hit by drought. Crops and animals can die of thirst. People may have to move somewhere else until it rains.

Spines also protect the lizard from enemies.

DID YOU KNOW?

The Atacama Desert in South America is the driest place on Earth. Some parts have had no rain for centuries. The Andes Mountains shield this region from the wet ocean winds.

The Sahara Desert

The Sahara Desert, which stretches across North Africa, is the world's largest desert. Plants, animals, and people have to be survival experts to live in this harsh place.

Sand dunes

About one fifth of the Sahara is covered in sand. The rest is covered in stones. The wind blows the sand into high hills called dunes. Saharan sand dunes look red at sunset.

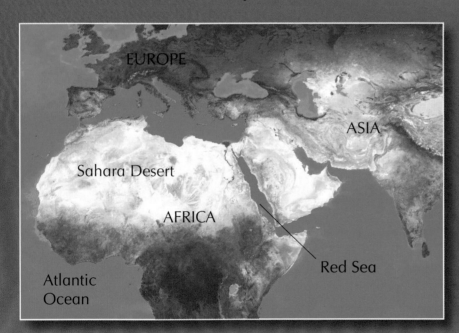

EUROPE

ASIA

Sahara Desert

AFRICA

Red Sea

Atlantic Ocean

World's biggest desert

This map shows the size of the Sahara. It stretches from the Red Sea to the Atlantic Ocean. The Sahara is actually getting bigger, as farmlands on the edge are hit by drought.

Sahara facts

- The Sahara is 3.5 million square miles (9 million sq km), an area the size of the United States.

- About 6,000 years ago, the Sahara was much wetter. Cave paintings show that elephants and giraffes once lived in areas that are now desert.

- The Sahara's tallest dunes are 1,525 feet (465 m) high.

Camels

In the Sahara, camels are used as pack animals. They carry goods and people across vast stretches of desert. When food is scarce, these tough animals live off the fat stored in their humps.

Broad hooves stop the camel sinking into the soft sand.

Desert people

Some people in the Sahara are nomads. They wander from camp to camp, sleeping in tents and leading their camels in search of food and water. Today, many desert nomads have settled down to live in towns.

Living with the weather

Furry hood and fleece jacket keep out icy winds.

All over the world, people have learned to cope with local weather conditions. The right clothes and the right type of home can keep people comfortable in scorching heat, bitter cold, or heavy rain.

Dressed for the cold

Some parts of the world have harsh winters with months of snow and ice. People dress in warm clothing when they go outside. Homes are cosy and well-heated.

Stilt houses have steep roofs that shed the rain.

Ready for floods

In regions that get heavy rain, flooding is common. In parts of Asia, some homes are built on stilts to keep them dry during floods. Small boats are used to travel about.

Cave homes

In deserts and places near the equator, the fierce heat can make life very uncomfortable. In parts of Africa and Australia, people keep cool in homes dug out of rock.

Hibernating animals

Animals have their own ways of dealing with harsh weather. Mammals, such as this groundhog, spend the winter months in a deep sleep called hibernation. Sleeping saves energy when food is scarce.

A hibernating groundhog.

187

Watching the weather

Weather plays a big part in our lives. It affects how we dress and whether we plan to be inside or outside. Knowing about the weather is especially important to farmers, sailors, and anyone who works outdoors.

Weather balloons send information by radio.

Weather balloon

Weather balloons measure conditions high in the atmosphere. They rise because they are filled with a light gas called helium. Aircraft and satellites also make records and watch out for storms.

DID YOU KNOW?

Weather stations aren't only found on land. They can also be ships at sea, floating buoys, or satellites in space. Weather stations file thousands of weather reports every day.

Weather stations

Weather stations all over the world measure rainfall, wind direction and speed, and air temperature—how warm or cold it is. These records are fed into computers, which help to work out what the weather will do next.

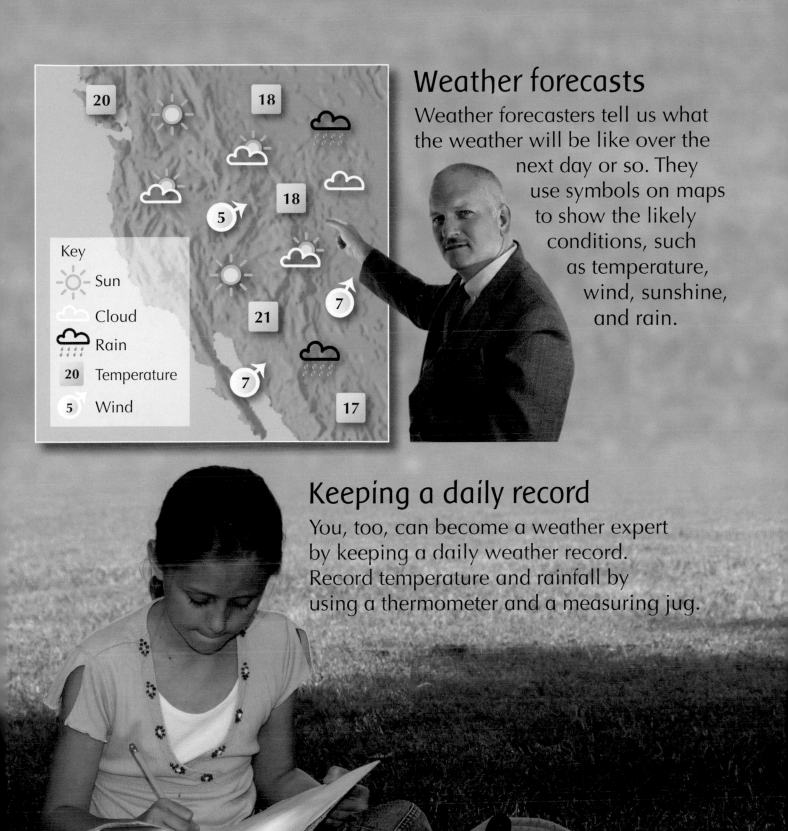

Weather forecasts

Weather forecasters tell us what the weather will be like over the next day or so. They use symbols on maps to show the likely conditions, such as temperature, wind, sunshine, and rain.

Key
- ☀ Sun
- ☁ Cloud
- 🌧 Rain
- 20 Temperature
- 5 Wind

Keeping a daily record

You, too, can become a weather expert by keeping a daily weather record. Record temperature and rainfall by using a thermometer and a measuring jug.

Wild weather

Most places on Earth are sometimes hit by severe weather, such as hurricanes, tornadoes, thunderstorms, hail, and heavy snow. This chapter explains the causes of wild weather—including how hurricanes form and why storm clouds produce hail or lightning. Experts say the world's weather is getting warmer and wilder. Read on to find out why and how we can take care of the Earth.

Hurricanes

Huge spinning storms with powerful winds are called hurricanes. The winds whirl about a calm "eye" in the center. Hurricanes form over warm oceans and cause damage when they hit land.

How do hurricanes form?

As the Sun heats the ocean, warm, moist air rises to form thunderclouds. Cold air rushes in at the bottom. The thunderclouds merge and start to spin.

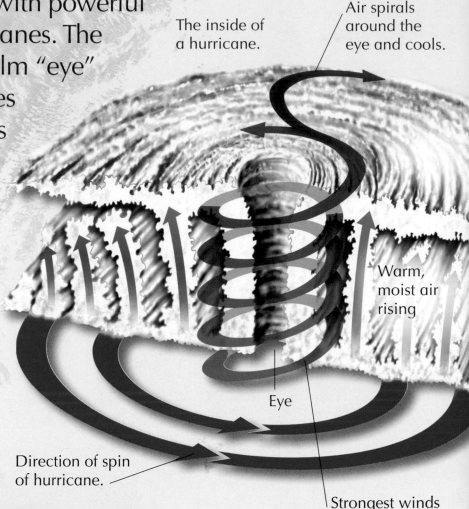

The inside of a hurricane.

Air spirals around the eye and cools.

Warm, moist air rising

Eye

Direction of spin of hurricane.

Strongest winds are around the eye.

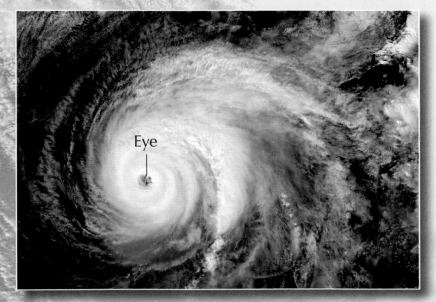

Eye

Whirling clouds

This picture of a hurricane was taken from space. It shows bands of cloud swirling around the eye in the center. Hurricanes are enormous—they can measure 300 to 500 miles (500 to 800 km) across.

Powerful winds

Hurricane winds blow at more than 185 miles (300 km) per hour. Whole trees can be uprooted. It is very dangerous to be outside in a hurricane.

DID YOU KNOW?

Fierce storms are called hurricanes if they form in the Atlantic Ocean. If they form in the western Pacific, they are called typhoons.

Hurricane damage

When hurricanes hit land, roaring winds can destroy homes and other buildings. These storms also bring heavy rain and can cause floods.

Hurricane Katrina

In 2005, a powerful hurricane called Hurricane Katrina struck the southern United States. The coastal city of New Orleans was badly flooded. It was the most destructive storm that has ever hit the United States.

Rising waters

Roaring winds, rough seas, and heavy rain caused flooding. The Mississippi River spilled over high banks called levees that had been built to prevent flooding. Water poured into the nearby city of New Orleans.

Wrecked towns

Hurricane Katrina wrecked seashore towns when it blew in off the ocean. Powerful winds tossed this truck into a tree. Boats were sucked out of the sea and hurled onto the shore.

Floodwaters burst through a levee.

Katrina facts

🌎 Winds up to 174 miles (280 km) per hour were recorded during Hurricane Katrina.

🌎 Floodwater covered four fifths of New Orleans. Homes, stores, and parks were covered by up to 20 feet (6 m) of water.

Boat rescue

City leaders ordered everyone to leave New Orleans. Helicopters and boats rescued people who had been stranded in their homes by the rising floodwater.

DID YOU KNOW?

During Hurricane Katrina, more than 1,000 people died. About 1 million homes were damaged by the high winds and flooding.

Returning home

When the water finally drained away, the levees were rebuilt. Damaged buildings then had to be repaired. It was a long time before it was safe for people to return to their homes. This family moved back a year later.

Tornadoes

Tornadoes are small but very violent storms. A whirling funnel of air weaves across the landscape, sucking up debris. Tornadoes form on land, not out at sea.

Twisting funnel can tower up to 650 feet (200 m) high.

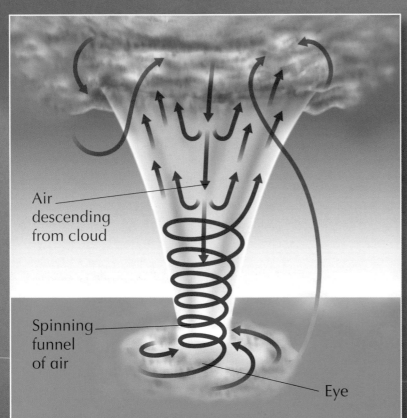

Air descending from cloud

Spinning funnel of air

Eye

Inside a tornado

Tornadoes are much smaller than hurricanes—usually less than ½ mile (1 km) across—but the winds inside whirl even faster. As in a hurricane, the winds spiral around a calm central "eye."

Touch down!

In hot, sticky weather, warm, moist air shoots upward to form towering thunderclouds. A funnel of whirling air appears below the cloud. It forms a tornado when it touches the ground.

Hit by a tornado

The superstrong winds of a tornado have tremendous power. But the path of destruction is usually narrow. A tornado may completely wreck one house but leave the next one untouched.

The damge caused by a tornado in Florida in 2007.

DID YOU KNOW?

Winds of about 373 miles (600 km) per hour have been recorded inside tornadoes. These are the fastest winds on Earth.

The tornado does a lot of damage where it touches the ground.

Tornado Alley

Tornadoes are most common in the United States. Each year, the country has about 1,000 tornadoes. Most form in an area called Tornado Alley (colored yellow on this map of the United States).

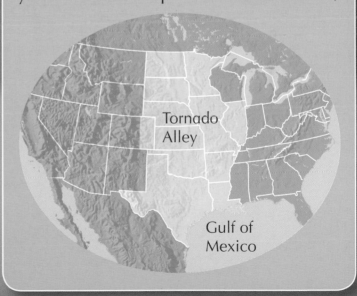

Tornado Alley

Gulf of Mexico

CANADA

New York

Michigan

Ohio

Indiana

West Virginia

Virginia

Illinois

Kentucky

North Carolina

UNITED STATES OF AMERICA

Tennessee

Mississippi

Alabama

Georgia

Tornado damage

Tornadoes travel only a short distance before dying out. But they leave a trail of destruction. Sometimes a whole group of tornadoes forms at once. This is called a tornado outbreak.

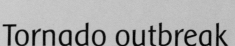

Tornado outbreak

In 1974, 148 tornadoes formed in a single day in the United States. The funnels swept across 13 states, as shown on the map. They killed 330 people and left a path of devastation 2,500 miles (4,000 km) long!

Tornado shelters

When a tornado strikes, the safest place to be is underground. Many homes in the United States have underground shelters in basements. People hide if they are told a tornado is due and come out when the danger has passed.

Freak damage

The funnel of a tornado acts like a giant vacuum cleaner. It can suck roofs off houses and flatten buildings. It can pick up cars like toys and toss them into the air.

DID YOU KNOW? Tornadoes have been known to pick up heavy objects. In 1931, a tornado lifted a train weighing 80 tons (88 tonnes), whirled it through the air, and threw it into a ditch.

Storm chasers

Most people will do anything to avoid a tornado. But experts called storm chasers enjoy watching tornadoes up close. When a tornado is reported, they race to the scene to photograph the storm.

Freak storms

Hurricanes and tornadoes are not the only spinning storms. Whirlwinds can form over the sea or whip up sand in deserts. These storms are usually small but scary.

Cloud of sand picked up by a dust devil.

Dust devils

Small tornadoes that form in deserts are called dust devils. The swirling air picks up sand and carries it up to 100 feet (30 m) in the air. Despite their name, dust devils don't usually do much harm.

Waterspouts

When a tornado strikes at sea, it forms a waterspout. The narrow, twisting funnel sucks up water and sometimes fish, too. If the waterspout moves on to the land, it may dump a shower of fish!

Funnel of whirling clouds hits the sea.

Shower of frogs!

Over the centuries, there have been many reports of animals or strange objects dropped by whirlwinds. In 1939, a shower of little frogs fell on a town in western England. Swirling winds had sucked the young frogs out of ponds.

Sandstorms

High winds can whip up sandstorms in deserts. Stinging sand fills the air, and people run for shelter. Wind can carry sand for thousands of miles and then dump it far away.

DID YOU KNOW?

In 1940, a shower of silver coins fell on the Russian town of Gorky. A whirlwind had carried off a hidden treasure chest, which then burst open, scattering coins.

A sandstorm in Pakistan has turned the sky orange.

Thunderstorms

About 2,000 thunderstorms rage somewhere on Earth every minute. These storms can cause terrible damage. They usually happen in hot weather, when warm, moist air rises to form thunderclouds.

What is lightning?

Swirling air in thunderclouds makes raindrops rub together. This produces tiny electric charges. Positive charges build up at the top of the cloud, negative charges build up at the bottom. Lightning sparks between the two.

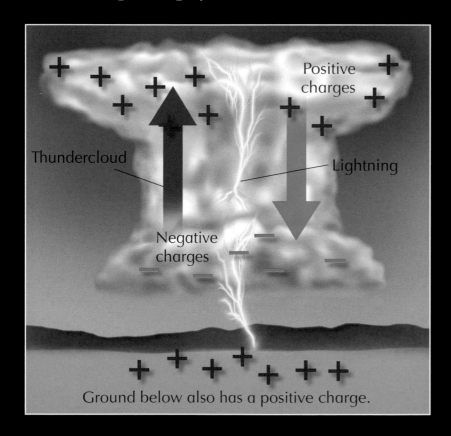

Positive charges

Thundercloud

Lightning

Negative charges

Ground below also has a positive charge.

Static electricity

The type of electricity that builds up inside thunderclouds is called static electricity. This is the same kind of electricity that makes your hair stand on end if you brush it hard!

Thunderclap

As lightning streaks through the sky, it heats the air to incredibly hot temperatures. The air explodes, causing a deafening crack of thunder. Light travels faster than sound, so you see the lightning before you hear the thunder.

DID YOU KNOW?

The sound of thunder takes five seconds to travel 1 mile (1.6 km). You can tell how far away a storm is by counting the seconds between the lightning and thunder and dividing the number by five.

Forest fires

Lightning can start forest fires, especially in dry weather. In 1988, fires caused by lightning raged through Yellowstone National Park. Many thousands of acres of forest were burned.

Streaks of lightning

Lightning is a huge spark of electricity. It can take different forms, depending on whether the spark flashes between clouds in the sky or shoots from a cloud to the ground below.

Sheet lightning

When lightning flashes between clouds, it produces sheet lightning. The sparks light up the clouds from inside, so they glow (as above).

Forked lightning hits a town in Utah.

Forked lightning

When lightning leaping downward splits into many branches, it is called forked lightning. Lightning flashes downward because the ground below has developed a positive charge.

Lightning strike

Lightning always takes the fastest route to the ground. Sparks are attracted to tall objects, such as trees and high buildings. For this reason, people should never shelter under a tree in a storm.

Lightning hits the lightning rod on a tall building in Shanghai, China.

Lightning rods

Tall buildings are often struck by lightning. A lightning rod makes the building safer. Lighting strikes the rod and then runs safely down a wire into the ground.

Monsoon and floods

In some parts of the world, winds called monsoons change direction in different seasons. Summer monsoons bring heavy rain, which can cause flooding.

Summer rain

Farmers rely on the monsoons to water their crops in summer. These farmers in India are planting rice during the monsoon rains.

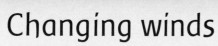

Changing winds

This diagram shows how monsoon rains in Asia change direction. In winter, winds blowing south from the mainland bring dry weather. In summer, winds blowing north off the ocean bring heavy rain.

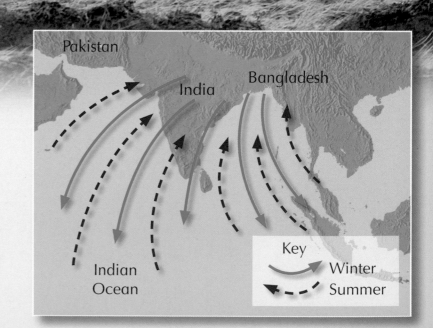

Pakistan

India

Bangladesh

Indian Ocean

Key

Winter

Summer

Hit by floods

Monsoon rains often cause floods
in Bangladesh, a low-lying country
next to India. Water flooded this
village in Bangladesh after
a heavy monsoon
in 2007.

DID YOU KNOW?

In 1900, the port of
Galveston, Texas, was
wrecked by floods during
a hurricane. A wall of
water swept right over the
town as the hurricane hit.

Storm surges

As a hurricane
moves over the sea,
it sucks up water.
The mound of water,
called a storm surge,
causes flooding when
it hits the coast.

Floodwater covered
this American
coastal town
following a
hurricane in 2003.

Snow and frost

In many parts of the world, winter brings frost, ice, and snow. If you wrap up warm, this wild weather can be a lot of fun!

Snow

Snow forms in clouds where the air is below freezing. The moisture in the clouds turns into ice crystals, which join to make snowflakes.

Snowflakes

All snowflakes have six points or six sides. No two flakes are the same shape. A scientist studied snowflakes for 50 years without ever finding two that were exactly alike!

Snow is good for going sledding.

Frost

In freezing weather, ice crystals form on leaves, windows, and other cold surfaces. We call these crystals frost. Thick frost can look like a coating of snow.

Icicles

Icicles may hang from roofs, trees, and cliffs in cold weather. They form when water starts to drip and then freezes. As more water trickles down and freezes, the icicles grow longer and longer.

DID YOU KNOW?

Paradise in Mount Rainier National Park is one of the world's snowiest places. One year, 105 feet (32 m) of snow fell on Paradise.

Hail and blizzards

Extreme winter weather can be dangerous. When heavy snow combines with strong winds, we call it a blizzard. Hail is when pellets of ice fall from the clouds.

Snowstorms

Swirling snow fills the air during a blizzard, and a layer of ice makes roads slippery. Roads can be blocked by the heavy snow.

Drivers cannot see far in a blizzard, which makes driving dangerous.

The plow blade pushes the snow out of the way.

How hail forms

Hailstones form when winds toss ice crystals up and down inside cold clouds. As the ice crystals rise and fall, more layers of ice are added, forming pellets of ice called hailstones. These hailstones eventually get so heavy they fall to the ground.

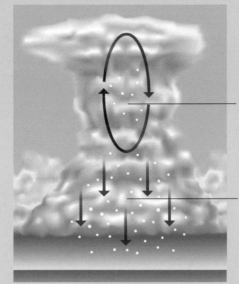

Hailstones are tossed up and down inside the cloud.

Heavy hailstones fall to the ground.

Most hailstones are about the size of a pea, but some can be much bigger.

Hail damage

Large hailstones do a lot of damage. Hailstones the size of baseballs can dent car roofs and smash windshields. They can also flatten crops.

Clearing snow

This snowplow is clearing a snowy road. Snow piles up on rooftops and branches during a blizzard. Trees, roofs, and even power lines can collapse under the weight of snow.

Changing weather

In recent years, wild weather has become much more common. Experts say that this is because the world is getting warmer and that harmful waste called pollution is to blame.

Global warming

Power stations burn coal, oil, and gas to provide energy. But they also release waste gases into the air. These gases are making Earth warmer—this is called global warming.

Greenhouse gases

Gases in the atmosphere trap some of the Sun's heat. They act like the glass in a greenhouse, so they are called greenhouse gases. Pollution is adding more of these gases into the air and this is making Earth warmer.

Sun

Some of the Sun's heat is trapped by gases in the atmosphere.

Atmosphere

Earth

Cars pump waste gas into the city air in Shanghai, China.

City pollution

Cars give off greenhouse gases. The air in cities is polluted by fumes from cars and factories. Cities cause a lot of pollution because so many people live there.

DID YOU KNOW?

Temperatures rose by about one degree during the twentieth century. Experts believe Earth may start to heat up more quickly if we don't reduce pollution now.

Melting ice sheets

Global warming is melting the ice in the polar regions. Melted ice is adding to the water in the oceans, making sea levels rise. This polar bear will have nowhere to hunt if all the ice melts.

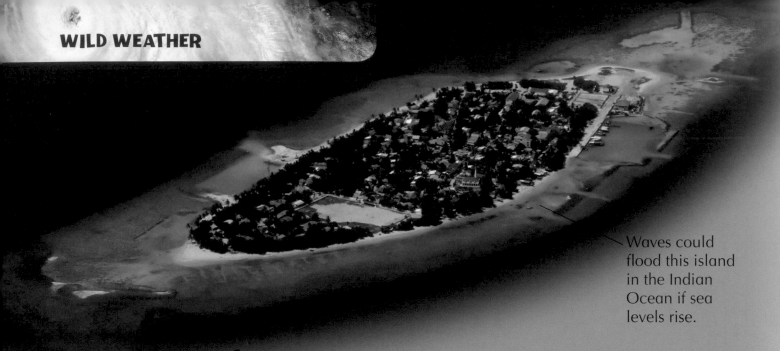

Waves could flood this island in the Indian Ocean if sea levels rise.

Caring for Earth

Global warming is making sea levels rise. It is also causing more wild weather. We need to find ways of reducing the pollution that is making Earth become warmer.

Rising seas

If sea levels carry on rising, cities by the coast could flood. Beautiful islands, such as the one above, could disappear. We need to produce less pollution to stop this happening.

Cycling

Car journeys cause a lot of pollution. We can produce far less pollution by choosing different ways to travel. People should try to walk, cycle, or take the train or bus to work or school.

Recycling

Waste paper, glass, metal, and plastic can be collected and sent to factories to be made into new materials. This is called recycling and helps to save energy.

A box of waste ready to be recycled.

Saving energy

Power stations that provide us with electricity are adding to global warming. We can help by using energy more carefully. People should switch off lights, televisions, and computers when they are not being used.

DID YOU KNOW?

Energy from the wind, Sun, and flowing water can be used to make electricity without causing pollution. These forms of energy are kind to Earth.

215

Some useful words

Air pressure
The weight of all the air pressing down on Earth.

Atmosphere
The layer of gases that surrounds Earth.

Aurora
Shimmering lights seen in the night sky at the North and South poles.

Axis
An imaginary line between the North and South poles. Earth rotates on its axis.

Biome
A large area of Earth's surface with a particular climate where the same types of plants grow.

Cell
One of the tiny units of which living things are made up.

Climate
The regular pattern of weather in an area.

Crater
A hollow in the ground or in the top of a volcano.

Crust
Earth's hard outer layer.

Crystal
A mineral with flat, smooth sides and a regular shape.

Delta
A flat area at a river's mouth made of sand or mud dropped by the river.

Drought
A period when no rain falls.

Equator
An imaginary line around the center of Earth.

Erosion
When rocks are worn away by the weather.

Eruption
When a volcano explodes ash and lava.

Estuary
The part of a river's course where it nears the sea.

Evacuation
When everyone has to leave an area to avoid danger.

Fault
A crack in Earth's crust formed by rocks shifting under the ground.

Fossil
The remains of ancient living things that have been preserved, usually as stone.

Fossil fuel
A fuel, such as coal or oil, made from the remains of prehistoric plants or animals.

Fuel
A substance that can be burned to give off heat and light.

Geyser
A hot underground spring that shoots out steam and boiling water.

Gills
The feathery parts on a fish's head used for breathing underwater.

Glacier
A huge mass of ice that slides slowly downhill.

Gravity
The pulling force of Earth, which makes things fall to the ground.

Greenhouse Effect
The warming effect produced by gases in the air that trap the Sun's heat.

Hemisphere
One half of Earth, as divided by the equator.

Humus
A layer on top of soil, made up of rotting plants.

Hurricane
A huge spinning storm with very strong winds.

Hydroelectric station
A place where electricity is made using energy from flowing water.

Ice Age
A period in the past when Earth's climate was much colder than it is today.

Lava
Magma that bursts out when a volcano erupts.

Levee
A high bank built along a river to prevent flooding.

Magma
Red-hot rock deep beneath Earth's crust.

Magnet
A piece of iron or steel that pulls iron and steel toward it.

Magnetic field
The area around a magnet that is affected by the magnet's pull.

Mantle
The thick layer inside Earth below the crust, where the rocks are red hot.

Meander
A bend or loop in a river.

Metal
A material, such as copper or gold, that is often shiny and can usually be shaped.

Mineral
A solid, natural material from which rocks are formed.

Monsoon
Winds that bring rain in the summer months in southern Asia.

North Pole
The most northerly point on Earth.

Oasis
A place in a desert where water is found.

Orbit
The path taken by a planet as it circles the Sun, or by a moon as it circles a planet.

Ore
A rock that contains a metal.

Photosynthesis
When plants use carbon dioxide, water, and sunlight to grow.

Plankton
Tiny plants and animals that float in the ocean.

Plate
One of the huge slabs of rock that make up Earth's crust.

Polar regions
The areas around the North and South poles.

Pollution
Any solid, liquid, or gas that harms nature.

Recycle
When materials, such as glass, metal, or plastic, are used again instead of being thrown away.

Seismograph
A machine used to measure the strength of earthquakes.

Smog
A dirty fog produced by pollution.

Solar system
The Sun and all the planets and rocks that circle around it.

South Pole
The most southerly point on Earth.

Spit
A long finger of land that sticks out into the sea.

Stack
A rocky pillar that stands in the sea.

Storm surge
A mound of water that forms in the ocean beneath a hurricane.

Temperate
An area with a mild climate.

Temperature
How hot or cold it is.

Tentacle
A long, armlike structure on an animal.

Thermal
A current of warm, rising air.

Tornado
A funnel of spinning air that forms beneath a thundercloud.

Tropics
The region around the equator where the climate is hot.

Tsunami
A giant wave caused by an earthquake or volcano.

Water vapor
Water in the form of a gas. When water is heated, it turns into water vapor. This is called evaporation.

WEB LINKS

Parragon does not accept responsibility for the content of any web sites mentioned in this publication. If you have any questions about their content, please refer to the organization that produced the web site. If you are under 18, the web sites mentioned should only be used with the involvement of a parent or guardian.

http://dsc.discovery.com/guides/planetearth/planetearth.html
Planet Earth section of the Discovery channel.

http://www.nationalgeographic.com
The National Geographic magazine.

http://kids.earth.nasa.gov/
NASA's Earth Science Enterprise web site for children.

http://www.nhm.ac.uk/kids-only/index.html
The children's section of the British Natural History Museum.

http://www.education.noaa.gov/students.html
The U.S. government weather site.

http://www.crh.noaa.gov
U.S. national weather service.

Index

Acknowledgments

Artwork supplied through the Art Agency by artists including Peter Bull and Myke Taylor. The Tyrannosaurus Rex on p24 supplied by Jon Hughes and Russell Gooday.

Photo credits:
b = bottom, t = top, r = right, l = left, m = middle

Cover images:
Front: br Kazuyoshi Nomachi/CORBIS, bm Kevin Schafer/CORBIS, bl Jenny E. Ross/CORBIS, m Bert Envision/CORBIS, tr Pixland/CORBIS, tm Staffan Widstrand/zefa/CORBIS, tl NASA/Roger Ressmeyer/CORBIS.
Back: bl moodboard/CORBIS, bm Gavin Hellier/GETTY IMAGES, tl NASA/CORBIS, tr Dietrich Rose/zefa/CORBIS.
Spine: NASA/CORBIS.

1 Digital Vision, 2–3 Dreamstime/Eugene Barzakovsky, 4–5 iStockphoto.com/Jan Will, 6tl Dreamstime.com/Boris Pamikov, 6ml Dreamstime.com/Dmytro Korolov, 6bl Dreamstime.com/Htuller, 6–7t Dreamstime.com/Yakobchuk, 6–7m Dreamstime.com/Wolfgang Amri, 6–7b iStockphoto.com/Andrew Martin, 7tl&bl Dreamstime.com/Gennadij Kurilin, 7tr Dreamstime.com/Stephen Mcsweeny, 7mr Dreamstime.com/Jose Fuente, 7br iStockphoto.com/Sergey Dubrovskiy, 8–9 Digital Vision, 10–11m NASA, 10 bl Dreamstime.com/Jinyoung Lee, 11tr Digital Vision, 11br iStockphoto.com/Soubrette, 12bl Dreamstime.com/Jeecis, 13tr Dreamstime.com/Ben Goode, 13br Dreamstime.com/Stephen Mcsweeny, 15tl Dreamstime.com/Jeanne Hatch, 15mr Corbis/Bernd Obermann, 15mlr Dreamstime.com/Geopappas, 15br Dreamstime.com/Koskins39, 16–17m Dreamstime.com/Sonya Etchison, 17b Dreamstime.com/Irochka, 18–19 NASA/JPL-Caltech, 19t Corbis/Bryan Allen, 19b Digital Vision, 20t Dreamstime.com/Ivan Cholakov, 20b iStockphoto.com/zbindere, 21b Dreamstime.com/Anthony Hall, 22 Dreamstime.com/Mark Bond, 23t Dreamstime.com/Ismael Montero, 23b Dreamstime.com/Kun Jiang, 25t Corbis/James L. Amos, 26 iStockphoto.com/Brett Hillyard, 27t Dreamstime.com/Joe Gough, 27b Dreamstime.com/Andrew Chambers, 29t Dreamstime.com/Musat Christian, 29b Dreamstime.com, 30t Dreamstime.com/Laurin Rinder, 30b Dreamstime.com/Nikhil Gangavane, 31t Dreamstime.com Dennis Sabo, 31b Dreamstime/Dennis Sabo, 32t Dreamstime.com/Maxfx, 32b Dreamstime.com/Roman Krochuk, 33t Dreamstime.com/Anthony Hathaway, 33b Dreamstime.com/Jan Martin Will, 34–35 Corbis/Herbert Spichtinger, 36t Dreamstime.com/Sebastian Kaulitzki, 36b Dreamstime.com, 37t Corbis/Ted Spiegel, 38t Dreamstime.com/Anatoly Tiplyashin, 38b Dreamstime.com/Charles Taylor, 39l Dreamstime.com/Peter Clark, 39r Dreamstime.com/Stephen Finn, 40t Dreamstime.com/David Lloyd, 40b Corbis/Robert Gill, 41t Dreamstime.com/Daniel Haller, 41b Dreamstime.com/Don Mace, 42t Dreamstime.com/David Lloyd, 42b iStockphoto.com/Carmen Martinez Banús, 43r Dreamstime.com/Rafael Laguillo, 43m Dreamstime.com/Andy Butler, 43b Dreamstime.com/Pavel Losevsky, 44t Dreamstime.com/Pancaketom, 44b Dreamstime.com/Jesse, 45t Dreamstime.com/Alexkalina, 45b Dreamstime.com/Aravindteki, 46 Dreamstime.com/Alena Yakusheva, 47t Dreamstime.com/Robert Cocquyt, 47m Dreamstime.com/Vlad Turchenko, 47b Dreamstime.com/David Watkins, 48l Dreamstime.com/Maxim Malevich, 48r Dreamstime.com/Kameel4u, 49t Dreamstime.com/Jerry Horn, 49b iStockphoto.com/Piotr Przeszlo, 50tl Corbis/Visuals Unlimited, 50tr Dreamstime.com/Andreasg, 50b Dreamstime.com/Kirill Bodrov, 51t Corbis/Bettmann, 51b Dreamstime.com/Oleg Fedorenko, 52l Corbis/Karen Michelmore, 52r Dreamstime.com/Ye Liew, 53t Dreamstime.com/Piotr Majka, 53m Corbis/Paul A. Souders, 53b Corbis/Jonathan Blair, 54t Dreamstime.com/Marat Hasanov, 55t Digital Vision, 55bl Dreamstime.com/Nicole Waring, 55bm Dreamstime.com/Evgeny Terentyev, 55br Dreamstime.com/Paul Butchard, 56l Dreamstime.com/Htuller, 57t Dreamstime.com/Alexandr Klochov, 57b iStockphoto.com/Donna Coleman, 58t Dreamstime.com/Pavel Gribkov, 58b Dreamstime.com/Phil Morley, 59t Dreamstime.com/Nikhil Gangavane, 59b Dreamstime.com/Alena Yakusheva, 60–61 Digital Vision, 62b Dreamstime.com/Sugarfree.sk, 63t Dreamstime.com/Marco Regalia, 63b Corbis/Michael S. Yamashita, 64b USGS/David Wieprecht, 65t Corbis/Jim Sugar, 65b USGS, 66–67 iStockphoto.com/Liz Leyden, 66t OAR/National Undersea Research Program (NURP), 66b Dreamstime.com/Simon Gurney, 67t Dreamstime.com/Keoni Dibelka, 68t USGS/Jim Nieland, 68b Corbis/Gary Braasch, 69t USGS/Lyn Topinka, 69b Dreamstime.com/Samuel Price, 70t Dreamstime.com/Victorpr, 70b Corbis/Sean Sexton, 71t Corbis/Les Stone/Sygma, 71b Corbis/Jacques Langevin/Sygma, 72t Corbis/Keren Su, 72b Dreamstime.com/Hugo Maes, 73t iStockphoto.com/Jeffrey Zavitski, 73b Dreamstime.com/Angela Cable, 74t Corbis/Roger Ressmeyer, 74b USGS/W. Chadwick, 75t Corbis/Les Stone/Sygma, 75b USGS/Gene Iwatsubo, 76 Dreamstime.com/Robert Paul Van Beets, 77t Corbis/Mark Downey/Lucid Images, 77b Corbis/TWPhoto, 78t NOAA/NGDC (National Geophysical Data Center), 78b Corbis/George Hall, 79t Corbis/Bernard Bisson/Sygma, 79b NGDC (National Geophysical Data Center), 80–81t Digital Vision, 80–81b iStockphoto.com/CK Lai, 81tr Corbis, 82t Corbis/Lisbon City Museum/Handout/Reuters, 82b USGS/Ralph O. Hotz, 83t Corbis/Peter Turnley, 83b Corbis/Warrick Page, 84t iStockphoto.com/James Benet, 84b Dreamstime.com/Adam Jastrzebowski, 85t Corbis/Reuters, 85b Dreamstime.com/Rafael Ramirez Lee, 86–87 iStockphoto.com/Vernon Wiley, 88t Corbis/Galen Rowell, 89b iStockphoto.com/Ogen Perry, 90 Dreamstime.com/Marc Johnson, 91t Dreamstime.com/Kevin Walsh, 91b iStockphoto.com/Warwick Lister-Kaye, 92–3 Dreamstime.com/Sascha Burkard, 93b Corbis/Skyscan, 94t Dreamstime.com/Jose Fuente, 94b Corbis/Robert Holmes, 95t iStockphoto.com/Robert Churchill, 95b Dreamstime.com/Jason Maeh, 96t Dreamstime.com/Alessandro Bolis, 96b Dreamstime.com/Andrew Millard, 97t Dreamstime.com/Robyn Mackenzie, 97b iStockphoto.com/Andrew Martin, 98t iStockphoto.com/Danny Warren, 99t iStockphoto.com/Marcella Francescangeli, 99b Dreamstime.com/Joeshmo, 100 Corbis/Steven Georges/Press-Telegram, 101tl Dreamstime.com/Mikel15, 101tr iStockphoto.com/Andreas Glossner, 101b iStockphoto.com/Nick Spannagel, 102t iStockphoto.com/Peter Archibald, 102b Dreamstime.com/Keith Young, 103t iStockphoto.com/Dmitry Pichugin, 103b Dreamstime.com/Jduggan, 104t iStockphoto.com/Ben Blankenburg, 104b Dreamstime.com/Stepanjezek, 105t Dreamstime.com/Mark Breck, 105b Corbis/Martin Harvey, 106–7 Dreamstime.com/Troy Farr, 106b Dreamstime.com/Joy Prescott, 107b Dreamstime.com/Reinhard Tiburzy, 108t Dreamstime.com/Spunky1234, 108b iStockphoto.com/Rey Rojo, 109t iStockphoto.com/Martin McCarthy, 109b iStockphoto.com/Bjorn Heller, 110t Dreamstime.com/Stephen Girimont, 110b Corbis/Arctic-Images, 111b Corbis/Johnathan Blair, 112–113 Digital Vision, 114t iStockphoto.com/Horst Puschmann, 115t iStockphoto.com/Roman Krochuk, 115b iStockphoto.com, 116–117 Dreamstime.com/Laurin Rinder, 116t Dreamstime.com/Laurie Weed, 117t iStockphoto.com/Sandra vom Stein, 117b Corbis/Ariel Skelley, 118t iStockphoto.com/Rob Jamieson, 119t iStockphoto.com/Milos Mokotar, 119b iStockphoto.com/Greg Brzezinski, 120t iStockphoto.com/Gregg Mack, 120b iStockphoto.com/Russell Gough, 121t Dreamstime.com/Ling Xia, 122l Jeff Schmaltz, MODIS Rapid Response Team, NASA/GSFC, 122b Wikipedia.org/Uryah, 123t iStockphoto.com, 123b Dreamstime.com/Jeffrey Banke, 124t Digital Vision, 124b USGS/National Center for EROS/NASA Landsat Project Science Office, 125t NASA, 125b Dreamstime.com/Gert Vrey, 126b iStockphoto.com,127t iStockphoto.com, 127b iStockphoto.com, 128t Corbis/Annie Griffiths Belt, 129t iStockphoto.com, 129b Corbis/Frank Lukasseck, 130t Dreamstime.com/Pierdelune, 130b Corbis/Ashley Cooper, 130–131m Dreamstime.com/Jhaviv, 131t Dreamstime.com/Aleksejs J., 131b Corbis/Pierre Vauthey, 132–133 Dreamstime.com/Vladimir Korostyshevskiy, 132m iStockphoto.com/Christopher Steer, 133t iStockphoto.com/Tom Grundy, 133m iStockphoto.com/Ian Scott, 134t iStockphoto.com/Edward Todd, 134b iStockphoto.com/Matthew Ragen, 135t iStockphoto.com/Alistair Scott, 135b Dreamstime.com/Olga Lyubkina, 136t Corbis/Hawes Alan/Sygma, 136b Corbis/Next Photo/Sygma, 137t iStockphoto.com/Geoffrey Hammond, 138–139 iStockphoto.com/James Steidl, 140t iStockphoto.com/Michael Braun, 141t iStockphoto.com/Natalia Diakov, 141b iStockphoto.com/Michael Steden, 142–143 Corbis/Rick Doyle, 143t Dreamstime.com/Jesse, 143m Dreamstime.com/Elisalocci, 144l iStockphoto.com, 144b iStockphoto.com/Michelle Reaves, 145t Dreamstime.com/Carolyne Pheora, 146t Edward Simkins, 146–147 iStockphoto.com/Rey Rojo, 147t Dreamstime.com/Nico Smit, 148t NASA, 148b iStockphoto.com/Vera Bogaerts, 149t Dreamstime.com/Wolfgang Amri, 149b iStockphoto.com/Trina Denner, 150l iStockphoto.com/Tammy Peluso, 151tr iStockphoto.com/Adrian Baddeley, 151m Dreamstime.com/Andrea Leone, 151b Dreamstime.com/Ian Scott, 152b Corbis/Douglas P. Wiilson/Frank Lane Picture Agency, 153t Corbis/Bob Gomel, 154m iStockphoto.com/Chris Zwaenepoel, 155t Dreamstime.com/Kiminnb, 156t Corbis/Ralph White, 156b OAR/National Undersea Research Program (NURP)/Woods Hole Oceanographic Inst., 157b Corbis/Ralph White, 158t Dreamstime.com/Pete Favelle, 158b Corbis/Tim Davis, 159b Corbis/Bettmann, 160t iStockphoto.com/Luis Pedrosa, 160b Corbis/Michael Freeman, 161t iStockphoto.com/Patricia Hofmeester, 161b Digital Vision, 162t Corbis/Bettmann, 162b iStockphoto.com/Kenneth C. Zirkel, 163t Corbis/Stephen Frink, 163b Dreamstime.com/Tatiana Edrenkina, 164–165 iStockphoto.com/Hans F. Meier, 166t Digital Vision, 167t Corbis/Nawang Sherpa/Bogati/ZUMA, 167b Dreamstime.com/Elena Elisseeva, 168t Dreamstime.com/Robyn Mackenzie, 168–169b Dreamstime/Eugene Barzakovsky, 169t iStockphoto.com/Barry Crossley, 169b iStockphoto.com, 170tl Dreamstime.com/Elena Schweite, 170tr Dreamstime.com/Aleksandr Ugorenkov, 170b Dreamstime.com/Millan, 171t Dreamstime.com/Paula Stephens, 171b Dreamstime.com/Boris Pamikov, 172t Dreamstime.com/Johann Helgason, 172b Dreamstime.com/Danijel Micka, 173l Dreamstime.com/Kurt, 173r Dreamstime.com/Dageldog, 174–175 Dreamstime.com/John Wollwerth, 174m Dreamstime.com/Kmitu, 175t iStockphoto.com, 175b iStockphoto.com/David Cannings-Bushell, 176–177t Dreamstime.com/Oleksandr Staroseltsev, 176b Dreamstime.com/Demydenko Myhailo, 177t Dreamstime.com/Yakobchuk, 177b Dreamstime.com/Jorge Salcedo, 178b Dreamstime.com/Douglas Hall, 179tr Dreamstime.com/Jörg Jahn, 179b Dreamstime.com/Dmytro Korolov, 180t Dreamstime.com/Viktor Ostashevskyy, 180b Dreamstime.com/Carolyne Pehora, 181t Dreamstime.com/Kjuby, 181b iStockphoto.com/Daniel Stein, 182l Dreamstime.com/Paul Moore, 182–183 Dreamstime.com/Roger Degen, 183t Dreamstime.com/Don Mace, 183m Corbis/Howard Burditt/Reuters, 184–185 Dreamstime.com/Vova Pomortzeff, 185t Dreamstime.com/Dmytro Korolov, 185b Corbis/Philippe Lissac/Godong, 186–187 iStockphoto.com/Sergey Dubrovskiy, 186b Corbis/Nik Wheeler, 187t Corbis/Wolfgang Kaehler, 187b iStockphoto.com/David P. Lewis, 188tl Dreamstime.com/Armin Rose, 188b Dreamstime.com/Millan, 189t iStockphoto.com/Lisa F. Young, 189b Dreamstime.com/Miflippo, 190–191 Corbis/Carson Ganci/Design Pics, 192b Jacques Descloitres, MODIS Rapid Response Team, NASA/GSFC, 193t Corbis/Daniel Aguilar/Reuters, 193b Melissa Ann Janssen/FEMA, 194t Marvin Nauman/FEMA, 194b Jocelyn Augustino/FEMA, 195t Bob McMillan/FEMA, 195b Mark Wolfe/FEMA, 196–197 Corbis/Eric Nguyen, 197t Mark Wolfe/FEMA, 198b John Plisich/ FEMA, 199t Andrea Booher/FEMA, 199b Corbis/Jim Reed, 200–201 iStockphoto.com/Christopher Walker, 200t iStockphoto.com/Vladimir Kondrachov, 201tl Dreamstime.com/Erik Lam, 201tr iStockphoto.com/Alexei Zaycev, 201b Corbis/Nadeem Khawer/epa, 202b iStockphoto.com/Mark Rose, 202–203t Digital Vision, 203b National Park Service, 204t Dreamstime.com/Alexander Zhiltsov, 204b iStockphoto.com/Michael Madsen, 205t iStockphoto.com/Lars Lentz, 205b Corbis/Reuters, 206t Corbis/Reuters, 207t Corbis, 207b Crystal Payton/FEMA, 208t Dreamstime.com/Gennadij Kurilin, 208–209 Dreamstime.com/Kathy Wynn, 209t Dreamstime.com/Anna Chelnokova, 209b Dreamstime.com/Georgy Pchemyan, 210t iStockphoto.com/Silvia Jansen, 210b iStockphoto.com/Rick Hinson, 211m Corbis/Jim Reed, 212b Digital Vision, 213t Dreamstime.com/Bertrandb, 213b iStockphoto.com/Jan Will, 214t Dreamstime.com/Kanu Suguro, 214b iStockphoto.com/Ana Abejon, 215l Dreamstime.com/Showface, 215r Dreamstime.com/Lukasz Fus.